Number 112
Winter 2006

New Directions for Evaluation

Promoting the Use of Government Evaluations in Policymaking

Rakesh Mohan
Kathleen Sullivan
Editors

PROMOTING THE USE OF GOVERNMENT EVALUATIONS IN POLICYMAKING
Rakesh Mohan, Kathleen Sullivan (eds.)
New Directions for Evaluation, no. 112
Jean A. King, Editor-in-Chief

Microfilm copies of issues and articles are available in 16mm and 35mm, as well as microfiche in 105mm, through University Microfilms Inc., 300 North Zeeb Road, Ann Arbor, Michigan 48106-1346.

New Directions for Evaluation is indexed in Cambridge Scientific Abstracts, Contents Pages in Education, Educational Research Abstracts Online, Higher Education Abstracts, Social Services Abstracts, Sociological Abstracts, and Worldwide Political Sciences Abstracts.

NEW DIRECTIONS FOR EVALUATION (ISSN 1097-6736, electronic ISSN 1534-875X) is part of The Jossey-Bass Education Series and is published quarterly by Wiley Subscription Services, Inc., A Wiley Company, at Jossey-Bass, 989 Market Street, San Francisco, California 94103-1741.

SUBSCRIPTIONS cost $80 for U.S./Canada/Mexico; $104 international. For institutions, agencies, and libraries, $199 U.S.; $239 Canada; $273 international. Prices subject to change.

EDITORIAL CORRESPONDENCE should be addressed to the Editor-in-Chief, Jean A. King, University of Minnesota, 330 Wulling Hall, 86 Pleasant Street SE, Minneapolis, MN 55455.

www.josseybass.com

Editorial Policy and Procedures

New Directions for Evaluation, a quarterly sourcebook, is an official publication of the American Evaluation Association. The journal publishes empirical, methodological, and theoretical works on all aspects of evaluation. A reflective approach to evaluation is an essential strand to be woven through every volume. The editors encourage volumes that have one of three foci: (1) craft volumes that present approaches, methods, or techniques that can be applied in evaluation practice, such as the use of templates, case studies, or survey research; (2) professional issue volumes that present issues of import for the field of evaluation, such as utilization of evaluation or locus of evaluation capacity; (3) societal issue volumes that draw out the implications of intellectual, social, or cultural developments for the field of evaluation, such as the women's movement, communitarianism, or multiculturalism. A wide range of substantive domains is appropriate for *New Directions for Evaluation;* however, the domains must be of interest to a large audience within the field of evaluation. We encourage a diversity of perspectives and experiences within each volume, as well as creative bridges between evaluation and other sectors of our collective lives.

The editors do not consider or publish unsolicited single manuscripts. Each issue of the journal is devoted to a single topic, with contributions solicited, organized, reviewed, and edited by a guest editor. Issues may take any of several forms, such as a series of related chapters, a debate, or a long article followed by brief critical commentaries. In all cases, the proposals must follow a specific format, which can be obtained from the editor-in-chief. These proposals are sent to members of the editorial board and to relevant substantive experts for peer review. The process may result in acceptance, a recommendation to revise and resubmit, or rejection. However, the editors are committed to working constructively with potential guest editors to help them develop acceptable proposals.

Jean A. King, Editor-in-Chief
University of Minnesota
330 Wulling Hall
86 Pleasant Street SE
Minneapolis, MN 55455
e-mail: kingx004@umn.edu

CONTENTS

EDITORS' NOTES 1
Rakesh Mohan, Kathleen Sullivan

1. Managing the Politics of Evaluation to Achieve Impact 7
Rakesh Mohan, Kathleen Sullivan
The authors examine issues in managing the politics of evaluation by considering the context in which an evaluation occurs and by maximizing both evaluators' independence from and their responsiveness to stakeholders.

2. A Voice Crying in the Wilderness: Legislative Oversight Agencies' Efforts to Achieve Utilization 25
Gary R. VanLandingham
The author contends that an emphasis on organizational independence can restrict evaluators' role to that of a voice crying in the wilderness rather than speaking truth to power.

3. Evaluators' Role in Facilitating the Convergence of Factors to Create Legislative Impact 41
Hal Greer
Using the example of Virginia's process of regulating the practice of medicine, the author concludes that evaluators can play an important role in facilitating the convergence of factors that can create legislative impact.

4. The Influence of Evaluators on State Medicaid Policies: Florida and South Carolina's Experience 51
Yvonne Bigos, Jennifer Johnson, Rae Hendlin, Steve Harkreader, Andrea Truitt
The authors describe environmental conditions and evaluation strategies that played a role in affecting Medicaid policies in two states.

5. A Utilization-Focused Approach to Evaluation by a Performance Audit Agency 67
Ron Perry, Bob Thomas, Elizabeth DuBois, Rob McGowan
The authors describe how evaluators can be involved in the development and implementation of management tools or models for the agency they evaluate while still maintaining their independence.

6. Using a Crystal Ball Instead of a Rear-View Mirror: Helping State Legislators Assess the Future Impacts of Major Federal Legislation 79
Joel Alter, John Patterson
Using prospective evaluation, the authors offer a rationale and methods for estimating future impacts of the No Child Left Behind Act.

7. Increasing Evaluation Use Among Policymakers Through Performance Measurement 89
Rakesh Mohan, Minakshi Tikoo, Stanley Capela, David J. Bernstein
The authors discuss a symbiotic relationship between performance measurement and evaluation, which has the potential to increase the use of evaluation among policymakers.

8. The Evaluator's Role in Policy Development 99
George F. Grob
Reflecting on his thirty-seven-year evaluation career in the federal government, the author discusses strategies for maintaining independence and credibility as an evaluator while also serving as an advocate for certain policy outcomes.

INDEX 109

EDITORS' NOTES

"We do not suffer from a lack of information here on Capitol Hill, but from a lack of ability to glean the knowledge and to gauge the validity, credibility, and usefulness of the large amounts of information and advice received on a daily basis" (U.S. House of Representatives, 2006). This is how U.S. Congressman Rush Holt of New Jersey described the information needs of policymakers at the federal level. He noted legislators' need for "assessments in a Congressional time-frame by those who are familiar with the functions, the language, and the workings of Congress" (U.S. House of Representatives, 2006). Although Holt's comments were specifically in reference to assessment of scientific and technical innovations, he clearly described a general need among policymakers for timely evaluative information reported in understandable language by unbiased sources. It is this need that evaluators at all levels of government, as well as those in many nonprofit organizations, seek to meet as they conduct evaluations, analyze policy options, and recommend action on the part of policymakers.

This volume focuses on the role of evaluators working in government settings in the United States, as well as in nonprofit organizations and private sector entities conducting evaluations on behalf of government. Federal, state, and local settings are considered together in this volume because the evaluation contexts within these settings bear many similarities. At each level of government, an elected legislative branch appropriates funds and oversees government programs and services administered by the executive branch. The legislative branch takes the form of a city or county council at the local level, a legislature or assembly at the state level, and a bicameral congress at the federal level. Evaluators at all three levels are aware of the sensitivity of the political environments in which they and their executive or legislative employers perform their work.

In addition to helping to improve the delivery of government services, these evaluators have an opportunity and a responsibility to help policymakers make informed decisions for the betterment of society. Evaluators' work, when used by policymakers, can have far-reaching fiscal and programmatic implications. This volume's chapter authors examine theoretical and practical approaches to designing evaluation projects in ways that promote the use of evaluation results in these high-stakes settings, where

---

The views expressed in these notes are those of the authors and do not necessarily represent those of the Office of Performance Evaluations or the Idaho legislature.

budgets range in the billions of dollars, even in the smallest states, and service recipients often number in the millions.

In considering evaluation use in democracies, Mark and Henry (2004) have likened evaluations to social interventions that produce outcomes. Evaluations that might lead to or away from social betterment are particularly relevant to the study of evaluation use (Henry and Mark, 2003). Several evaluators contributing to this volume offer examples of evaluations that policymakers used in promoting social betterment and share strategies to increase evaluation use among policymakers. Before introducing their stories of evaluation use, we first consider what constitutes evaluation use by policymakers.

In two chapters, the authors suggest categories of evaluation use by policymakers. Because these categories include direct and indirect changes set in motion by an evaluation, they might be considered forms of the "evaluation influence" described by Mark and Henry (2004; Henry and Mark, 2003). However, because the concept of influence is relatively new, the chapter authors have used the more widely known categorization. Citing a series of utilization categories drawn from the research literature, Gary VanLandingham in Chapter Two describes evaluation use as instrumental when it occurs through policymakers' implementation of recommendations, enlightenment producing when it influences policymakers' thinking over time, process related when learning on the part of stakeholders and others occurs through participation in the evaluation, and symbolic when policymakers use evaluation to justify decisions made earlier about a program.

In Chapter Four, Yvonne Bigos, Jennifer Johnson, Rae Hendlin, Steve Harkreader, and Andrea Truitt mention the most readily observable type of utilization within a government policymaking context: legislators' adoption of evaluation recommendations through enactment of statutes or modification of budgets. These examples of an evaluation's direct influence on policy can be placed in Mark and Henry's collective category of influence, which includes evaluations that result in policy change (Mark and Henry, 2004; Henry and Mark, 2003). More subtle forms of evaluation use described by Bigos and others in Chapter Four include policymakers' formation of ad hoc groups, such as select legislative committees, to focus attention on an issue; requests that evaluation offices conduct additional studies, such as supplemental fiscal analyses; and references to evaluation findings in legislative debates. These evaluation utilization behaviors are examples of a category Mark and Henry designated interpersonal influence, which occurs when "an evaluation's findings are used to persuade others about the merit of a program or policy" (Coffman, 2005, p. 11). Henry also describes an individual form of influence, which occurs when the "thoughts, attitudes, beliefs, or actions" of policymakers have been influenced by an evaluation (Coffman, 2005, p. 11). External forms of use (collective or interpersonal) might occur after the individual form of influence has affected the thinking of one or more policymakers.

None of these forms of influence can take place if policymakers are uninterested in the work that evaluators produce. A broadly recognized need for responsiveness to issues of importance to key stakeholders (Patton, 1997) to promote utilization raises the question of independence. Can evaluators perform their work independently while responding to these stakeholder needs? In Chapter One, we acknowledge the intrinsically political nature of evaluation and note that evaluations are not conducted in a vacuum. The only option evaluators and evaluation organizations have is to manage the politics of evaluation. We also examine issues in managing the politics of evaluation by considering the context in which an evaluation occurs and examining strategies for maximizing both evaluators' independence from and their responsiveness to key stakeholders.

When evaluations influence the decisions of policymakers in any of the ways discussed in Chapters Two and Four, evaluators' work can have far-reaching fiscal and programmatic implications. Recognizing what some may consider the low rate at which evaluators' recommendations are adopted by policymakers, VanLandingham illustrates the applicability of utilization-focused evaluation strategies that are relevant to evaluation work within a variety of governmental and nongovernmental settings. He also includes a review of literature on utilization challenges that evaluators face, including the political nature of evaluation environments and the challenges of communicating through written reports in institutional environments in which personal relationships and informal interaction are more valued than written analysis. Limited use of evaluation work produced by legislative oversight offices may be explained by the fact that many of these offices do not use strategies that the evaluation use literature suggests when conducting and reporting their work. Utilization strategies that are particularly relevant to legislative environments include obtaining input from key legislative stakeholders to ensure that evaluation work meets legislative information needs and appropriately designing and marketing the work to legislative decision makers.

The balance of the chapters demonstrate the feasibility of incorporating utilization-focused practices into evaluations conducted in government settings by offering examples of projects in which evaluators have used such strategies with varying levels of success. For example, in Chapter Three, Hal Greer, an evaluator working in a legislative oversight agency, describes the uneven pace of policy change that occurred in response to an evaluation of a medical licensure board found to be ineffective in protecting the public from harm by practitioners. Greer explains factors associated with the evaluation's ultimate influence on public policy. One of the strategies used to promote utilization of the evaluation was the evaluators' establishment of report credibility through a carefully implemented research process. The evaluators also promoted utilization through a clearly written report that effectively identified the problem and recommended a solution.

In Chapter Four, a group of legislative oversight evaluators from two states describe evaluations of critical components of their states' Medicaid programs, including prescription drug provisions and prevention of fraud and abuse. They explore critical conditions that played a role in influencing legislative action in Florida and South Carolina and describe factors affecting the implementation or lack of use of report recommendations by these legislative bodies. Factors they consider related to legislatures' implementation of recommendations include legislative input in identifying critical issues and project scope; political and public interest and influences that support a climate of change; and presentation of feasible, practical, and cost-effective policy alternatives.

Chapters Five and Six discuss the promise offered by a prospective approach in the analysis of programmatic and fiscal impact. The authors of these chapters, which describe an operational cost model for correctional agency budgeting (Chapter Five) and a series of simulations and surveys to anticipate the fiscal and programmatic impact of the federal No Child Left Behind (NCLB) legislation (Chapter Six), discuss the features of their studies that policymakers found to be most useful. Ron Perry, Bob Thomas, Elizabeth DuBois, and Rob McGowan, the authors of Chapter Five, describe the King County, Washington, performance audit agency's development of an operational cost model that can be used as an analytical tool by the correctional agency, as well as for the performance audit agency's ongoing oversight and review of county jail operations. The project they describe illustrates evaluators' enhancement of the relevance and utility of the work of the performance audit agency while maintaining the agency's role as a provider of government oversight. The authors draw a parallel between their work with their county's correctional agency and a new emphasis on prospective analysis on the part of agencies such as the U.S. Government Accountability Office. By using a prospective approach, county performance auditors oriented their evaluation results toward implementation while strengthening management capabilities within a government agency. Similarly, Joel Alter and John Patterson, the authors of Chapter Six, used quantitative methods and a prospective approach to examine the likely impact of NCLB. The authors of both chapters note that prospective evaluations, or the evaluation of hypothesized or likely future impacts, can play an important role in providing credible, useful information to policymakers.

Chapter Seven deals with performance measurement, which policymakers at all levels of government use as an accountability tool. Authors Rakesh Mohan, Minakshi Tikoo, Stanley Capela, and David Bernstein suggest that evaluators consider the potential for a symbiotic relationship between performance measurement and evaluation. Evaluation methods can be used to help design a sound performance measurement system, which can provide evaluators with performance criteria and data for assessing a program's impact. By explaining the respective functions of performance measurement and evaluation to policymakers, evaluators potentially can increase the use of evaluation by helping policymakers formulate questions raised by performance data, such as why a program works or does not work, and by explaining evaluation's role in answering these questions.

Although the evaluators who contributed these chapters mention their reports' inclusion of recommendations for use by policymakers, most do not identify themselves as policy analysts. Nevertheless, policymaking is among the major uses of evaluation. Three functions through which an evaluation may lead to social betterment are determination of the common good, as well as selecting and adapting courses of action (Henry, 2003), all of them components of policymaking.

Moving beyond policy analysis to active advocacy for specific policy positions, George Grob discusses a range of policy roles in the final chapter. Basing his observations on wisdom garnered through his thirty-seven years of federal government service, Grob maintains that an evaluator's effectiveness in a government setting is contingent on mastery of policy analysis skills, as well as knowledge of professional ethics and a practical understanding of advocacy for a policy outcome within the boundaries of evaluation practice and professional ethics. Because an evaluator typically strives toward independence, the role of the evaluator as advocate is a departure from the norm. Adoption of the advocate role presents challenges in resolving this apparent conflict of interest. Grob asserts that the independence of the evaluator is valued by policymakers and that one of the most effective ways to ensure use of policy-related evaluations is to legitimately preserve the evaluator's reputation for independence. He discusses strategies for maintaining independence and credibility as an objective evaluator while serving as an advocate for certain policy outcomes. Whether it is influencing the implementation and future directions of national issues like Medicaid and NCLB or effecting change at the local level by strengthening the state medical licensure board and improving oversight and operation of the county jail, these are examples of how evaluation can be used for the betterment of the society.

We are grateful to editor-in-chief Jean King and associate editor Nancy Zajano for their thoughtful consideration of the ideas we presented in planning and preparing this volume, as well as for their valuable suggestions for improving the work of all chapter authors. We also thank Idaho's Joint Legislative Oversight Committee and the staff of Idaho's Office of Performance Evaluations for their work on reports from which examples were derived to illustrate points in Chapters One and Seven.

Rakesh Mohan
Kathleen Sullivan
Editors

References

Coffman, J. "A Conversation with Gary Henry." *Evaluation Exchange,* 2005, *11,* 10–11.

Henry, G. T. "Influential Evaluations." *American Journal of Evaluation,* 2003, *24,* 515–524.

Henry, G. T., and Mark, M. M. "Beyond Use: Understanding Evaluation's Influence on Attitudes and Actions." *American Journal of Evaluation,* 2003, *24,* 293–314.

Mark, M. M., and Henry, G. T. "The Mechanisms and Outcomes of Evaluation Influence." *Evaluation,* 2004, *10*(1), 35–57.

Patton, M. Q. *Utilization-Focused Evaluation.* (3rd ed.) Thousand Oaks, Calif.: Sage, 1997.

U.S. House of Representatives. Committee on Science. Democratic Caucus. "Congress Needs Access to Best Possible Scientific Information." July 25, 2006. Retrieved Aug. 23, 2006, from http://sciencedems.house.gov/press/PRArticle.aspx?NewsID=1171.

RAKESH MOHAN is director of the Office of Performance Evaluations of the Idaho legislature.

KATHLEEN SULLIVAN, now retired, was professor and director of the Center for Educational Research and Evaluation at the University of Mississippi.

1

This chapter examines issues in managing the politics of evaluation by considering the context in which an evaluation occurs and by maximizing both evaluators' independence from and their responsiveness to stakeholders.

Managing the Politics of Evaluation to Achieve Impact

Rakesh Mohan, Kathleen Sullivan

Should evaluators care about the impact of evaluation on the public policy process? If the larger purpose of evaluation is social betterment, the public-policy arena affords tremendous opportunities for evaluators to have both short- and long-term impact by influencing policy formulation, implementation, and outcomes (Henry, 2000; Henry and Mark, 2003; Mark, Henry, and Julnes, 2000). Working in the public policy arena inevitably involves coming in contact with politics, which raises two questions. First, should evaluators avoid politics? After all, evaluators are expected to provide independent assessment of policies and programs. Often this expectation implies that evaluators can insulate themselves from the politics of their environment; political entanglement is something to be avoided. Second, can they conduct evaluation in a vacuum devoid of any politics and still be effective in influencing the public policy process?

Evaluation Without Politics: A Reality Check

Whether by force, persuasion, intimidation, or inspiration, "A getting B to do H" is considered central to a political event (Frohock, 1974, p. 382). Although this central proposition has been well established, not so readily

The views expressed in this article are those of the authors and do not necessarily represent those of the Office of Performance Evaluations or the Idaho legislature.

WILEY InterScience® DISCOVER SOMETHING GREAT

NEW DIRECTIONS FOR EVALUATION, no. 112, Winter 2006 © Wiley Periodicals, Inc.
Published online in Wiley InterScience (www.interscience.wiley.com) • DOI: 10.1002/ev.204

determined are the specific characteristics of an event described as political, a term that can range in meaning from "involving the state or its government" to "based on or motivated by partisan or self-serving objectives" (*Random House Unabridged Dictionary,* 2006). Similarly, the term *politics* can be construed as "the art or science of government or governing," or it can have a more sinister meaning, such as "intrigue or maneuvering within a political unit or group in order to gain control or power" (*The American Heritage Dictionary of the English Language,* 2004). "Exercising or seeking power" (*Random House Unabridged Dictionary,* 2006) is a component of yet another definition of *politics.*

In examining the politics of evaluation, Palumbo (1987) considered the pejorative view of the term *politics,* but chose to use a definition that conveyed a more neutral meaning that extends well beyond narrow partisan activities. In his discussion of evaluation and politics, Palumbo considered politics to be "the interactions of various actors within and among bureaucracies, clients, interest groups, private organizations and legislatures as they relate to each other from different positions of power, influence, and authority" (pp. 18–19). Palumbo's broad definition underlies the term *politics* as we use it in this chapter.

Evaluation is intrinsically political (Palumbo, 1987). The very programs that evaluators examine are "creatures of political decisions" (p. 47); even initiation or sponsorship of an evaluation can be a political act (Weiss, 1987). Evaluation findings, which are reported for decision-making purposes, are considered within the political arena, and in advocating for a recommendation, the evaluator takes on an activist role in promoting social change (Iriti, Bickel, and Nelson, 2005). In Chapter Eight of this volume, Grob discusses in depth the evaluator's role as an advocate and its implications for evaluator independence and credibility.

Political decision-making processes can include consideration of evaluators' recommendations in the shaping of public policy, which is sometimes seen as the culmination of evaluators' efforts (Patton, 1997). Several of the chapters that follow illustrate policymakers' eventual use of evaluation results following evaluators' efforts to employ specific strategies aimed at promoting utilization. Examples of successful outcomes following use of these strategies are legislative utilization of evaluators' recommendations to strengthen Virginia's regulation of the practice of medicine, described in Chapter Three, and the use of evaluators' recommendations to improve the efficiency of South Carolina's and Florida's Medicaid programs, described in Chapter Four.

Many points of intersection between evaluation and politics occur long before the completed evaluation report is conveyed to the sponsoring policymaker. Some of these intersections occur during the evaluation's planning and implementation stages. For example, Patton (2003) noted that in the evaluator's selection of cases appropriate to the evaluation's purposes and resources, he or she might sample some politically important cases to attract attention to the evaluation. Alternatively, the evaluator might prefer to avoid attracting undesired attention by "purposefully eliminating politically sensitive cases from the sample" (p. 5).

Although evaluation practice is infused with political considerations, post hoc use of evaluation findings occupies a central position in social researchers' understanding of the politics of evaluation (Taylor, 2005). Evaluators who work hard to preserve the scientific integrity of carefully controlled randomized studies may, of course, find that policymakers use the results of their evaluations for political purposes, including partisan uses (Palumbo, 1987). But Palumbo (1987) observed that virtually all participants in social interaction are partisans. Even if policy analysts are respectful, responsible, and broad-minded, their work is a component of the political process, and they exert an influence only through participation in that process. Furthermore, Palumbo recognized the relationship between evaluators' values and their work and considered the values of researchers to be "part and parcel of their research" (p. 29). Thus, evaluators cannot stand apart from the political environment or from their own biases.

If "A getting B to do H" lies at the heart of a political event, evaluation indeed is fraught with political complexity. Service recipients attempt to "get" (Frohock, 1974, p. 382) program personnel to tailor programs to meet their needs, possibly by getting evaluators to get policymakers to get program personnel to do so. During an evaluation project, agency and program personnel attempt to get evaluators to report to policymakers findings that will cast their programs in a favorable light. Later, evaluators attempt to get policymakers and agency personnel to act on evaluators' findings and recommendations, while policymakers attempt to get public approval by getting agency and program personnel to improve program efficiency and effectiveness. In a constantly changing political environment within a democratic, pluralistic society, evaluators are challenged to promote use of their work by managing the politics of all these attempts at persuasion.

Understanding the Evaluation Environment

The first step in managing the politics of evaluation is to understand the evaluation environment. Patton has recommended that evaluators understand the evaluation's political context and consider how these political factors might affect the eventual use of the evaluation (Patton, 2002). In his Key Evaluation Checklist, Scriven (2006) recommended identifying the political considerations underlying the program's purpose. If the evaluation environment is disregarded, not even the most methodologically sound evaluation is likely to have an impact on the public policy process. To be effective, evaluators need to recognize various political forces, identify key players (both sponsors of the evaluation and other stakeholders who have some stake in the outcome of the evaluation), and understand interactions among those players, who often have competing and conflicting interests in the larger evaluation environment (Mohan, Bernstein, and Whitsett, 2002).

In addition to knowing who the key players are, evaluators need to understand what these players want from the evaluation and when they want that information (Grasso, 2003). Such knowledge helps evaluators effectively plan and conduct the evaluation, as well as disseminate the evaluation results in a timely manner. The challenge, of course, lies in sorting and prioritizing those wants as they relate to the scope of the evaluation. Involving the potential users in the evaluation process is the best way to encourage use of evaluation (Weiss, 1998).

The evaluation environment is often larger and more complex than some evaluators view it. As shown in Figure 1.1, the limited view of the evaluation environment includes a few entities shown inside the circle: the evaluation office, the entity overseeing the evaluation office, the agency under review and its clients, and relevant boards and commissions that oversee the agency under review. However, in the real world, the wall of that limited evaluation environment is porous, allowing penetration by the outside world's influences and disruption of the presumed harmony among a few stakeholders. For example, at the state level, the outside forces include the governor and his or her staff, legislative leadership, legislative committees and staff, individual legislators, professional associations, and the press. Similar evaluation environments with varying degrees of complexity exist at the federal and local levels.

Figure 1.1. Public Policy Evaluation Environment

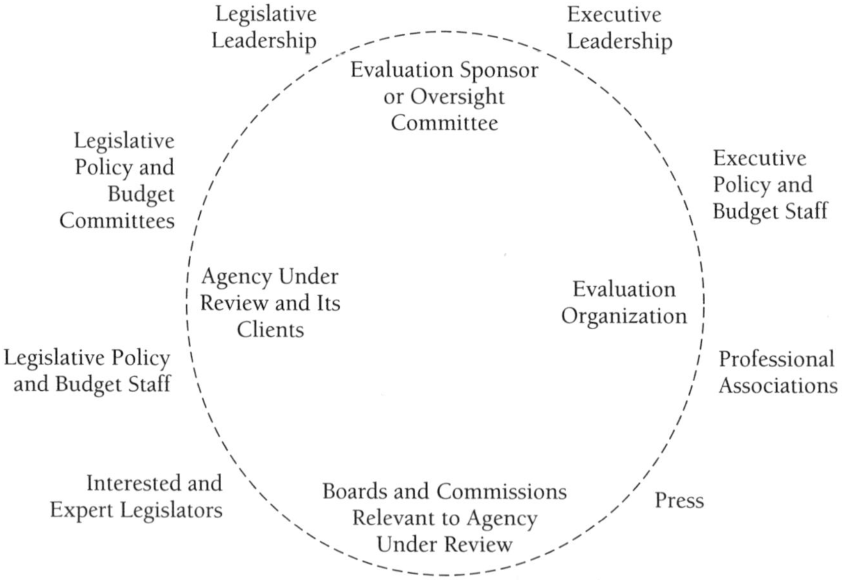

Maximizing Both Independence and Responsiveness

The evaluation literature shows that being responsive to stakeholders helps to increase evaluation use (Patton, 1997). Responsiveness inevitably brings evaluators closer to their stakeholders, which may blur the line that keeps the evaluator at arm's length and provides the independence necessary for maintaining credibility. Some evaluation standards—in particular, those used by evaluators working in and for government oversight agencies—place heavy emphasis on being independent from stakeholders as a means to achieve credibility. Although these standards serve evaluators well in achieving credibility, they often create a distance between the evaluators and the stakeholders. As a result, responsiveness to stakeholders is often compromised. Some agencies address this by maintaining a balance between independence and responsiveness. For example, an evaluator who is attempting to be responsive to policymakers' information needs might carefully review a transcript of a meeting in which legislators discussed conditions surrounding the need for an evaluation. However, in the interest of independence, he or she might just as carefully avoid face-to-face discussions with legislators on the evaluation questions to be answered. A better approach might be for evaluation agencies to try their best to maximize both independence and responsiveness simultaneously, because we cannot trade one for the other. In essence, we lose credibility if we are not independent, and we conduct evaluations that are not useful if we are not responsive.

Figure 1.2 schematically shows four groups of evaluators, varying in their emphasis on independence and responsiveness based on their organizational culture (Mohan, 2003). There are no clear guidelines as to what constitutes independence and responsiveness; both fall on a continuum. Independence, in the strictest sense, means to some that the evaluators have no stake—in either fact or appearance—in the outcome of the evaluation or in whether evaluation findings and recommendations are used. However, if evaluators' ultimate goal is to work toward the betterment of society, it will be natural for evaluators to have some interest in the outcome of the evaluation and whether anyone uses the evaluation information. Similarly, responsiveness has different meanings to different people. For example, if an evaluator completes the evaluation assignment he or she was given and delivers the report on time to the sponsors of the evaluation, some would consider that evaluator to be fully responsive. However, others would expect the evaluator to be responsive to other stakeholders, beyond the sponsors. Chapter Five of this volume provides a good illustration of how the evaluators of the King County Auditor's Office in Seattle, Washington, maximized both independence and responsiveness while conducting their jail studies.

One way to determine whether an evaluator is both independent from and responsive to the sponsors and stakeholders is through assessing how

Figure 1.2. Independence from and Responsiveness to Sponsors and Stakeholders

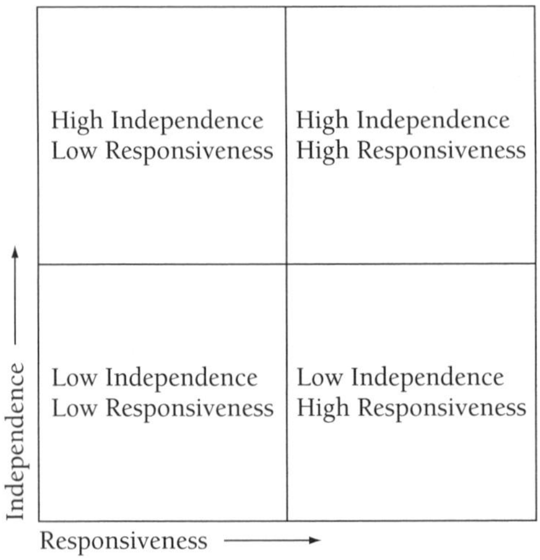

Strategies for Maximizing Both

- Consider the political context
- Consult extensively with policymakers
- Identify key stakeholders
- Understand the relationships among stakeholders
- Respond to stakeholders' needs
- Manage the project's scope
- Appreciate and respond appropriately to policymakers' timing constraints
- Exercise statutory authority to have access to data judiciously
- Use evaluation methods that produce accurate information based on a broad range of perspectives
- Prepare reports that are balanced in content and tone
- Use professional standards to guide the evaluation work

the evaluation was used. Absence of either will have a negative impact on evaluation use. In her 1995 presidential address to the joint conference of the American Evaluation Association and the Canadian Evaluation Society, Eleanor Chelimsky said, "Evaluators' survival in a political environment depends heavily on their credibility, as does the use of their findings in policy" (Chelimsky, 1995, p. 219). As we discuss later in this chapter, evaluation utilization strategies that help maximize both independence and responsiveness include identifying key stakeholders; understanding the political context, including the relationships among key stakeholders; consulting with and responding to the needs of sponsors and stakeholders; managing the project's scope; appreciating and responding appropriately to the timing constraints under which policymakers operate; judiciously exercising statutory authority providing access to data; using evaluation methods that produce accurate information based on a broad range of perspectives; using professional standards to guide the evaluation work; and preparing reports that are balanced in content and tone.

Clearly it is more challenging and risky to attempt to maximize both independence and responsiveness, because this effort brings the evaluator into close proximity with stakeholders and their politics. Nevertheless, the rewards for such an endeavor are also obvious: seeing the fruits of one's labor when policymakers use evaluation results. When evaluators are attempting to maximize both independence and responsiveness, professional standards are useful in guiding their conduct and the evaluation activities. There are three sets of commonly used evaluation standards in the United States: Guiding Principles for Evaluators (American Evaluation Association, 2004), the Program Evaluation Standards (Joint Committee on Standards for Educational Evaluation, 1994), and the Government Auditing Standards, commonly known as the Yellow Book (U.S. Government Accountability Office, 2003).

The choice of standards depends primarily on government and professional requirements, organizational culture, and the professional backgrounds of evaluators (Mohan, 1997; National Conference of State Legislatures, 2004). For example, evaluators and performance auditors working in government settings often use the Government Auditing Standards, and those working in the field of education tend to use the Program Evaluation Standards. In Chapter Two, VanLandingham mentions characteristics of two types of legislative evaluation offices: those that primarily use Government Auditing Standards and those that use other evaluation standards. All three sets of standards nevertheless agree on evaluation essentials:

- Involving stakeholders
- Maintaining independence and disclosing conflicts of interest
- Using sufficient and credible evidence to support findings, conclusions, and recommendations
- Protecting confidentiality of certain information
- Using a quality assurance process
- Presenting a balanced report
- Keeping records to demonstrate that proper evaluation methods were used

These standards differ from each other with respect to the degree of focus they place on some evaluation-related issues, including evaluators' independence and stakeholder involvement. For example, the Government Auditing Standards place a heavy emphasis on evaluators' independence, and the Guiding Principles and the Program Evaluation Standards are more focused on stakeholder involvement. (It should be noted that none of these standards are in conflict with each other with respect to independence and stakeholder involvement.) Practices used in complying with these standards might more accurately be described as locations along a continuum than as binary choices mandated by opposing standards. Furthermore, regardless of what these standards say, it is practitioners whose interpretations of these standards shape how evaluations are carried out. Where an evaluator or an evaluation agency falls on the continuum shown in Figure 1.2 will depend on how these standards are interpreted.

How to Maximize Both Independence and Responsiveness

The following four vignettes are from work that was done between 2003 and 2006 by Idaho's Office of Performance Evaluations, an independent legislative agency responsible for promoting confidence and accountability in government through its evaluations of state agencies and programs. The office works under the general direction of the bipartisan Joint Legislative Oversight Committee, an eight-member committee divided equally between the two major political parties and the two chambers of the legislature. The oversight committee's main responsibility is to assign evaluation projects to the office of nine staff. (One of the authors of this chapter, Rakesh Mohan, is the director of this office. The use of *I, me, we, us,* and *our* in these vignettes refers to Mohan and his office.) All of the studies discussed in these vignettes are available on the office's Web site (www.idaho.gov/ope).

Public Education Studies. During the 2003 legislative session in Idaho, a year of budget shortfalls, legislative leadership was interested in finding ways to improve efficiencies in public education, which accounted for about half of the state's general fund budget. Legislative leaders asked our office to conduct a performance evaluation of three school districts, with a focus on identifying cost savings, and complete the study before the end of the session. This meant we had only two months to complete the study. In their request, they asked us to focus specifically on fifteen items related to analyzing the use of various funds and expenditure categories such as transportation, technology, and building maintenance (see the evaluation request in appendix A, Idaho Legislature, 2003).

This request came a little more than two months after I had assumed my position as director of the office. I was new to the legislature and to the state; neither the legislature nor public education officials knew much about me. I had yet to establish my credibility as someone who could be responsive to the legislature's information needs and stay independent in the eyes of stakeholders. This large and nebulous assignment called for a review of the entire K–12 public education system and determination of where money goes and what efficiencies could be realized. Furthermore, public education touches many stakeholders and is one of the most highly visible and political areas of public policy. The request presented several additional challenges: (1) considering the resources available to the office, it seemed an impossible task to complete in two months; (2) there were questions regarding the appropriateness of the methodology that would involve selecting only 3 of the state's 114 districts; and (3) we did not know how we would be received by local school districts, since neither our office nor the legislative financial audits office had conducted an oversight review of local districts in more than a decade. I felt that my and the office's future depended on how I responded to the leadership request for delivery of something that would be meaningful and timely and that lawmakers would find useful, and how I would accomplish this while staying true to my profession as an independent evaluator.

We proposed to the leadership a more manageable multiphased approach for conducting the study over a period of approximately one year. The first phase involved quickly reviewing the revenue and expenditure data submitted by school districts to the Idaho State Department of Education and other states' data compiled by the National Center for Educational Statistics. We communicated with all major stakeholder groups—legislators, the Board of Education, the Idaho Department of Education, school districts, and various professional associations serving school district administrators, teachers, and parents—to gain their support and cooperation for the study. We analyzed the available data and presented our analysis to the legislature during the session, providing legislators and the public a more transparent view of education finances within five weeks of the request. Although we were not able to identify areas of cost savings as originally requested by legislative leadership, our report helped legislators focus on areas of public education administration that needed most attention. They were able to use our report to request two studies for the second phase of the project: one on accountability for expenditure of pupil transportation funds and another on the general administration and oversight of school districts (Idaho Legislature, 2004a, 2004b). Results of these studies were reported at the start of the 2004 legislative session, about nine months after the first report was issued. The 2004 legislature used our findings and recommendations to make statutory and budgetary changes; it passed five pieces of legislation related to topics examined in our reports.

By breaking the monolithic study into three smaller studies and spreading them over a year, we were able to (1) study the issues in depth and use appropriate research methods; (2) report our findings and recommendations to lawmakers in a timely manner, allowing them to use the information in making policy and budget decisions; and (3) prevent possible criticism from stakeholders that we were biased or, worse, involved in a witch-hunt that was likely to emerge had we selected only three districts to do our analysis. Being both responsive and independent in this case meant that we laid out all of the facts about our resources and limitations to the legislative leadership, sought their input, and negotiated a time frame that met their needs as well as ours in terms of conducting a study that was methodologically sound and defensible. Key elements of the methodology included consulting with all stakeholders, selecting a much larger number of districts (twenty-three) to conduct detailed site visits, analyzing an extensive amount of school district financial data, and reviewing best practices within and outside Idaho.

Idaho School for the Deaf and the Blind. This evaluation was assigned to us at a time when the legislature was concerned about the school's decreasing enrollment and rising costs per student. In addition, there was talk about closing the school and terminating residential services.

From the evaluation request, media coverage, and our background research, we learned that the evaluation involved stakeholders who had competing and conflicting interests. Once again, politics was at the forefront, and there was no escape from it if the office was to conduct the study. Specifically, we had to manage and appropriately respond to three challenges:

1. Those who supported the use of assisted technologies, such as cochlear implants in teaching hearing-impaired students, were at odds with those who believed in preserving Deaf culture by emphasizing the use of sign language only. Passions were high on both sides.
2. School staff were facing some morale issues involving the school's interim superintendent. Some of the staff did not support the vision and goals of the superintendent and remained loyal to the previous superintendent.
3. In the town of Gooding, where the school is located, people were saying that the school would be shut down, causing apprehension and fear among school staff and those who lived in the community. The school is a major employer in this small community.

In light of this background, stakeholder involvement became the backbone of our methodology. Not only did we remain independent and neutral, we had to ensure that all involved parties perceived us as such. "You can be the peacemaker," said the chair of the House Education Committee. He explained the context of the evaluation request and the recent history of the school and said that our study would benefit the school and the legislature if we approached it correctly. He went on to explain what he meant by the "correct" study approach: sensitivity to the prevailing cultures of the school and its clients, inclusion of input from all stakeholders, clear focus, and total independence in conducting the study. We heeded his advice and designed our study to include the following components:

- Surveying all special education directors in the state, interviewing many members of school staff, and conducting group interviews with school teachers and outreach workers to understand the issues in depth and establish trust.
- Interviewing a physician who performed cochlear implant surgeries in Idaho and other professionals who had knowledge about the use of assisted technologies.
- Conducting a focus group with parents who supported the use of assisted technologies and did not subscribe to the philosophy of teaching only sign language to their sensory-impaired children.
- Surveying parents of all students enrolled at the school's main and satellite campuses and a random sample of parents (45 percent of the population) whose children received outreach services. We translated surveys in Spanish for parents who spoke Spanish as their first language.

- Using sign language interpreters for focus groups and our report presentations to meet the needs of some of our stakeholders. We also published our report in braille. Although these were small steps in our methodology, they were extremely important in establishing our credibility as independent evaluators who were sensitive to the needs of the sensory-impaired population.
- Using consultants to review our report drafts to ensure our research methods were appropriate; analyses, conclusions, and recommendations were logical and based on solid evidence; and our report was balanced and sensitive to Deaf culture and to those who supported the use of assisted technologies. Consultants included a professor of evaluation at Gallaudet University, an institution for deaf and blind students; a professor of educational research and evaluation; and a professor of psychology specializing in research methods. They not only provided technical comments that were helpful in improving the quality of our report, but also lent credibility to our report.

We issued our report prior to the 2006 legislative session so lawmakers could use the information in making policy and budget decisions during the session. The report concluded the school was at a turning point—declining enrollment, rising costs per student, campus facilities used at less than one-half capacity, and increasing demand for regional services—and policymakers needed to determine its future (Idaho Legislature, 2005).

The report made a significant impact on the policy process. The information was helpful to lawmakers in setting the school's fiscal year 2007 appropriations and passing a bill that would help improve services to sensory-impaired children. In addition, the report served as a catalyst for an ongoing debate on how to address the long-term needs of sensory-impaired students. A bill changing the current model of providing education to sensory-impaired students was introduced but did not pass. A committee of the state Board of Education was formed to study the feasibility of various options, and the legislature is expected to discuss this issue again during the 2007 legislative session.

Our methodology allowed us to involve all stakeholders and obtain perspectives of diverse groups of stakeholders. We responded to all of the questions that were asked of us by the legislature, and all parties saw the report as a credible piece of work:

"Your report points out issues that will require serious debate in order to come to a proper course of action for the future of the school" (governor's response to the evaluation, Idaho Legislature, 2005, p. 77).

"The courteous and thorough manner in which you and your staff conducted this review has certainly been a key to its successful outcome" (Board of Education's response to the evaluation, Idaho Legislature, 2005, p. 79).

"There was an outstanding cooperative effort on the report," said the school's interim superintendent at the October 17, 2005, meeting of the Joint Legislative Oversight Committee (meeting minutes available at www.idaho.gov/ope).

The cooperation between the Office of Performance Evaluations and the school was "stellar," commented one of the co-chairs of the Joint Legislative Oversight Committee at its October 17, 2005, meeting (meeting minutes available at www.idaho.gov/ope).

Health and Welfare Management. At the October 17, 2005, meeting of the Joint Legislative Oversight Committee, I had two choices: (1) tell my committee that the office could not conduct a broad-scope study of the Department of Health and Welfare's management due to lack of time and resources, or (2) find a way to narrow the scope of the study to allow completion in four months, in time for lawmakers to use the information during the 2006 legislative session. If we were going to be responsive to the legislature's information need, the first option was not acceptable. Hence, we set out to pursue the second option.

At the October meeting, we presented the scope of our study of the management of the state's largest agency, with an annual budget of approximately $1.6 billion and staff of more than three thousand full-time positions. We proposed a multiphase approach to our committee. The purpose of the first phase was to understand how well department management was doing with respect to some of its key functions: external communication with policymakers and stakeholders, internal communication with staff, and workload distribution. In addition, the first phase was to identify areas needing further review in phase two. The methodology for the study had these components:

- Surveying all line staff and supervisors
- Surveying all program managers and middle managers
- Reviewing the department's methods for managing its caseloads, workloads, and staffing
- Analyzing the department's turnover rate

We decided to survey all employees because we did not want to leave any doubts as to whether the survey results were reflective of the entire population. To accomplish this mammoth task, we used a Web-based survey, which eliminated the need for entering survey responses into a database and checking the accuracy of that database. In order to accomplish our study objectives quickly, we used every resource that was available to us: our entire office worked on the project, and we enlisted the help of six consultants. The consultants helped by providing us extra hands to carry out needed tasks, ensuring the quality of our report, and lending credibility to our report.

We worked closely with key legislators and legislative budget and policy staff to make sure we clearly understood the legislative concerns about the department's management. There was no time on this project to make any adjustments to our course of action had we gone off track. We issued our report on February 28, 2006, four months and eleven days after the oversight committee approved the scope for the study (Idaho Legislature, 2006a). Because of the limited focus and the use of targeted methodology, we were able to provide useful information to policymakers. The report led to the following changes:

- Statutory changes to strengthen the role of the Board of Health and Welfare that provides general oversight to the department
- Establishment of a legislative interim committee to study issues relating to the department's mental health and substance abuse programs
- Organizational changes in the department by the governor
- Ongoing internal review of the department based on the areas identified in the report for further study

Idaho Student Information Management System. This vignette adds a new dimension to the evaluation environment in which a private, nonprofit foundation was a major player. In response to legislative concerns, the Joint Legislative Oversight Committee directed us to review the failed Idaho Student Information Management System (ISIMS) to determine what lessons could be learned for future information technology projects (Idaho Legislature, 2006b). ISIMS was a partnership between the state and a private, nonprofit foundation that had pledged $35 million to the state for developing a statewide student information management system for the K–12 public education system. The foundation terminated the project in December 2004, citing project cost overruns estimated to be $182 million.

In addition to having the involvement of a private foundation, the other monumental challenge was to review a high-profile project that had failed in a very public way. In some people's minds, the question was whether this evaluation was going to be a finger-pointing exercise. We recognized the nature of our assignment early on and made it clear that the purpose of the evaluation was to identify lessons that could be applied to the state's future information technology efforts, not to assign blame for failures. To understand what worked and did not work during the planning and implementation of the ISIMS project, we worked with a broad range of stakeholders: legislators and legislative staff, as well as officials of the governor's office, the Board of Education, the Department of Education, school districts, and the private foundation. We interviewed or surveyed state staff and private contractors who worked on the ISIMS project, which allowed us to understand the complexities of the project and the interactions among those stakeholders and helped us to inform key players about the nature of our evaluation and its progress.

Another challenge we faced was in obtaining documents that were deemed proprietary by the private foundation. The foundation "retains ownership of all intellectual property designed or purchased for the ISIMS project, including documentation" (Idaho Legislature, 2006b, p. 4). Because the foundation declined our requests for project documentation, we could not review in detail the management structures of the foundation or its contractors or validate the foundation's cost estimates cited as the reason for terminating the project. Since our objective was to identify lessons that could benefit the state when considering information technology projects in the future, we elected to pursue alternative sources of information rather than formally contest the foundation's decision to withhold information from us on proprietary grounds. Although we could have asked our oversight committee to exercise its statutory authority to issue subpoenas, we elected not to do so. Instead, we obtained the information by visiting school districts and surveying and interviewing many department and school district staff, former consultants, and vendors who had been involved with the project. Had we taken the path of formally contesting the foundation's decision, we could have gotten bogged down in the politics of the study instead of managing them. Because we used many alternative sources and methods to obtain the information, we believe the information withheld by the foundation would not have altered our conclusions.

We identified five lessons from our review of the failed information management project:

- Consider local and regional differences when developing a statewide information management system.
- Clearly define roles and responsibilities for all parties involved with the project.
- Involve end users of technology in project planning.
- Have realistic expectations of technology and understand its limitations.
- Be sure the project scope is manageable and time frames are realistic.

These lessons are applicable to any technology project, not just those in the area of education. Based on these lessons, we developed a best practices checklist for state agencies to use when undertaking information technology projects. Because our report was issued six months prior to the start of the 2007 legislative session, we do not yet know the legislative impact of our report. However, only a few weeks after we issued the report, the governor sent a letter to ninety-five state elected officials, administrators, and department and division heads encouraging them to use our checklist of best practices when considering information technology projects. The state's Information Technology Resource Management Council also adopted the checklist as a guideline for state agencies to follow.

Conclusion

In each of the four projects, the evaluation staff maximized responsiveness in these ways:

- Consulted extensively with policymakers to identify their evaluation questions and other information needs
- Considered the political context, such as agency sensitivity to issues that were the focus of the evaluation
- Identified and understood the relationships among key stakeholders
- Managed the project's scope to ensure feasibility of completion within the available time frame
- Responded to sponsors' and stakeholders' information needs
- Carefully assessed the pros and cons of obtaining certain information through exercising statutory authority of the evaluation office
- Used professional standards to guide the evaluation work

The staff maximized independence by using evaluation methods that yielded accurate information based on a broad range of perspectives and prepared reports that were balanced in content and tone. Instead of ignoring the politics of evaluation and pretending to be immune to politics, evaluators in these examples faced the reality that evaluators "are constrained by the context of the study, the politics of the setting, and even the politics of the government" (House, 2004, p. 7).

Eliciting information from stakeholders with diverse value sets paradoxically contributes to evaluators' independence by reminding us that our own values exist among a diverse set of stakeholder perceptions. We hone our independence as we examine the logic of our findings and recommendations in light of stakeholder perceptions. In the late 1990s, amid evaluators' calls for advancing the positions of some stakeholders, particularly the least powerful, Chelimsky (1998) warned that active advocacy—which might be manifested in an evaluator's attempt to use evaluation specifically to promote the interests of disadvantaged people, for example, or through reluctance to report that a social program does not work—can undermine the utilization of an evaluation product. Distinguishing between achieving an understanding of program beneficiaries' views and actively championing those views, Chelimsky noted that it is through a position of impartiality that an evaluation report gains prestige in public debates.

References

American Evaluation Association. *The Guiding Principles for Evaluators.* Fairhaven, Mass.: American Evaluation Association, 2004. Retrieved Dec. 31, 2006, from www.eval.org.

The American Heritage Dictionary of the English Language. (4th ed.) Boston: Houghton Mifflin, 2004. Retrieved Sept. 4, 2006, from http://dictionary.reference.com/search?q=political.

Chelimsky, E. "The Political Environment of Evaluation and What It Means for the Development of the Field." *American Journal of Evaluation,* 1995, *16,* 215–225.
Chelimsky, E. "The Role of Experience in Formulating Theories of Evaluation Practice." *American Journal of Evaluation,* 1998, *19,* 35–55.
Frohock, F. M. "Notes on the Concept of Politics: Weber, Easton, Strauss." *Journal of Politics,* 1974, *36,* 379–408.
Grasso, P. G. "What Makes an Evaluation Useful? Reflections from Experience in Large Organizations." *American Journal of Evaluation,* 2003, *24,* 507–514.
Henry, G. T. "Why Not Use?" In V. J. Caracelli and H. Preskill (eds.), *The Expanding Scope of Evaluation Use.* New Directions for Evaluation, no. 88. San Francisco: Jossey-Bass, 2000.
Henry, G. T., and Mark, M. M. "Beyond Use: Understanding Evaluation's Influence on Attitudes and Actions." *American Journal of Evaluation,* 2003, *24,* 293–314.
House, E. R. "The Role of the Evaluator in a Political World." *Canadian Journal of Program Evaluation,* 2004, *19,* 1–16.
Idaho Legislature. *Overview of School District Revenues and Expenditures.* Boise, Idaho: Office of Performance Evaluations, 2003.
Idaho Legislature. *Fiscal Accountability of Pupil Transportation.* Boise, Idaho: Office of Performance Evaluations, 2004a.
Idaho Legislature. *School District Administration and Oversight.* Boise, Idaho: Office of Performance Evaluations, 2004b.
Idaho Legislature. *Idaho School for the Deaf and the Blind.* Boise, Idaho: Office of Performance Evaluations, 2005.
Idaho Legislature. *Management in the Department of Health and Welfare.* Boise, Idaho: Office of Performance Evaluations, 2006a.
Idaho Legislature. *Idaho Student Information Management System (ISIMS)—Lessons for Future Technology Projects.* Boise, Idaho: Office of Performance Evaluations, 2006b.
Iriti, J. E., Bickel, W. E., and Nelson, C. A. "Using Recommendations in Evaluation: A Decision-Making Framework for Evaluators." *American Journal of Evaluation,* 2005, *26,* 464–479.
Joint Committee on Standards for Educational Evaluation. *The Program Evaluation Standards.* (2nd ed.) Thousand Oaks, Calif.: Sage, 1994.
Mark, M. M., Henry, G. T., and Julnes, G. *Evaluation: An Integrated Framework for Understanding, Guiding, and Improving Policies and Programs.* San Francisco: Jossey-Bass, 2000.
Mohan, R. "Legislative Evaluators: A Diverse Group of Professionals." *NLPES News,* Sept. 1997. Retrieved on Dec. 31, 2006, from http://www.ncsl.org /programs/nlpes/news/news0997.htm#view.
Mohan, R. "Surviving My First Legislative Session." *NLPES News,* Spring–Summer 2003. Retrieved on Dec. 31, 2006, from http://www.ncsl.org /programs/nlpes/news/news0603.pdf.
Mohan, R., Bernstein, D. J., and Whitsett, M. D. (eds.). *Responding to Sponsors and Stakeholders in Complex Evaluation Environments.* New Directions for Evaluation, no. 95. San Francisco: Jossey-Bass, 2002.
National Conference of State Legislatures. National Legislative Program Evaluation Society. *Ensuring the Public Trust.* Denver: National Conference of State Legislatures, 2004.
Palumbo, D. J. "Politics and Evaluation." In D. J. Palumbo (ed.), *The Politics of Program Evaluation.* Thousand Oaks, Calif.: Sage, 1987.
Patton, M. Q. *Utilization-Focused Evaluation: The New Century Text.* (3rd ed.) Thousand Oaks, Calif.: Sage, 1997.
Patton, M. Q. "Utilization-Focused Evaluation Checklist." 2002. Retrieved Sept. 20, 2006, from http://www.wmich.edu/evalctr/checklists/ufe.pdf.
Patton, M. Q. "Qualitative Evaluation Checklist." 2003. Retrieved Sept. 20, 2006, from http://www.wmich.edu/evalctr/checklists/qec.pdf.

Random House Unabridged Dictionary. New York: Random House, 2006. Retrieved Sept. 4, 2006, from http: //dictionary.reference.com/search?q=political.

Scriven, M. S. "Key Evaluation Checklist." 2006. Retrieved Sept. 20, 2006, from http://www.wmich.edu/evalctr/checklists/kec_june06.pdf.

Taylor, D. "Governing Through Evidence: Participation and Power in Policy Evaluation." *Journal of Social Policy*, 2005, *34*, 601–618.

U.S. Government Accountability Office. *Government Auditing Standards*. Washington, D.C.: U.S. Government Printing Office, 2003.

Weiss, C. H. "Where Politics and Evaluation Research Meet." In D. J. Palumbo (ed.), *The Politics of Program Evaluation*. Thousand Oaks, Calif.: Sage, 1987.

Weiss, C. H. "Have We Learned Anything New About the Use of Evaluation?" *American Journal of Evaluation*, 1998, *19*, 21–34.

RAKESH MOHAN is director of the Office of Performance Evaluations of the Idaho legislature.

KATHLEEN SULLIVAN, now retired, was professor and director of the Center for Educational Research and Evaluation at the University of Mississippi.

2

Although evaluation utilization literature has identified a wide range of practical actions that evaluators can take to maximize use of their work by policymakers, an emphasis on organizational independence can limit use of these strategies. This can restrict evaluators' role to that of a voice crying in the wilderness rather than speaking truth to power.

A Voice Crying in the Wilderness: Legislative Oversight Agencies' Efforts to Achieve Utilization

Gary R. VanLandingham

State legislatures face many challenges in carrying out their constitutional duties, including reconciling the conflicting demands made by diverse groups, balancing budgets in the face of rapidly rising costs for health care and security, and responding to challenges to improve education, transportation, and other essential services, all while keeping taxes low to promote economic competitiveness.

Scholars who have studied legislatures using economic theory have categorized these challenges into two primary forms of risk. First, legislatures face information limitations that hinder their budgeting and policymaking actions. They operate in an uncertain and complex environment (Gilligan and Krehbiel, 1987, 1989) and have limited time and information to make decisions (Epstein and O'Halloran, 1999). They have become a primary source of policy innovation in the United States, yet they often lack information on the effectiveness of their policy innovations (Jonas, 1999). Legislators, who tend to be generalists given the wide range of policy problems they face, are also at a disadvantage when dealing with executive branch agencies that have much more specialized knowledge about individual programs but may also be protecting their own interests (Moe, 1989).

The views expressed in this article are the author's and do not necessarily reflect those of the Florida legislature.

WILEY InterScience® DISCOVER SOMETHING GREAT

NEW DIRECTIONS FOR EVALUATION, no. 112, Winter 2006 © Wiley Periodicals, Inc.
Published online in Wiley InterScience (www.interscience.wiley.com) • DOI: 10.1002/ev.205

When faced with policy choices, legislators often have limited information about the options and their consequences (Knight, 1996).

Second, legislatures face substantial challenges ensuring that the policies that they create are faithfully implemented by the executive branch. They have limited ability to ensure that agencies carry out policies and use funds in the manner intended (Horn, 1995; Epstein and O'Halloran, 1994, 1999). McCubbins, Noll, and Weingast (1989) termed this risk "bureaucratic drift," as agencies can pursue their own goals regardless of those intended by the enacting legislators. While legislators can provide some control against bureaucratic drift by carefully designing programs and limiting agencies' discretion in carrying them out, this is often impracticable due to time and political constraints.

These problems are exacerbated by the increasing demands being placed on state legislatures. Over the past thirty years, the responsibilities of legislatures have expanded dramatically as the federal government has devolved authority to states in areas such as public assistance and environmental regulation (Osborne, 1990; Tubbesing, 1999). At the same time, legislatures are encountering growing internal stresses due to historic shifts in partisan and ideological control of governments (National Conference of State Legislatures, 2004a), ongoing budget crises (National Conference of State Legislatures, 2003), and demographic shifts arising from the increasing ethnic diversity of the population and the aging of the baby boomer generation (Ingraham, 1995).

Using Evaluation to Address Challenges Facing Legislatures

To address these challenges, legislatures can use several tools, including holding committee meetings to receive testimony, conducting special investigations, and relying on interest groups and the media to alert them to problems (Wohlstetter, 1990; McCubbins and Schwartz, 1984). One of the potentially strongest oversight tools is the work of legislative evaluation units (A. Rich, personal communication, Apr. 3, 2006).

Most state legislatures have created these offices; nationwide surveys have identified forty-three such offices (VanLandingham, 2004). (Two states have established multiple units: the Bureau of State Audits and the Legislative Analyst in California and the Texas Sunset Commission and the State Auditor in Texas.) These nonpartisan offices are charged with speaking truth to power (Wildavsky, 1979) by providing analysis to support the legislative process. Their function is typically similar to that of the U.S. Government Accountability Office, Congress's primary federal oversight unit, in that the offices report directly to elected legislators but typically have some organizational independence. These offices conduct policy analyses that identify and assess policy alternatives, program audits and evaluations that assess whether enacted programs are achieving desired goals in a manner consistent with legislative intent, and investigations of alleged agency misfeasance and malfeasance (Bezruki, Mueller, and McKim, 1999; Jonas, 1999; National Conference of State Legislatures, 2002).

In some states, these units are organized as an independent legislative office, and in others they are part of a legislative committee or a subunit of a legislative auditor that also performs financial audits (VanLandingham, 2004). Nationwide, these offices have approximately 840 staff researchers who represent a broad variety of academic disciplines, including political science, public administration, law, business studies, sociology, and natural sciences (VanLandingham, 2001, 2004). Legislatures typically have given these units almost unique access to governmental information, including nonpublic records such as tax returns; some units also have subpoena powers to force agencies to provide desired information (Jonas, 1999).

Examining the Impact of Evaluation

Given their location within the legislative branch, extensive resources, and broad access to information, these offices have the potential to play a critical role in helping legislatures manage the information and commitment challenges of budgeting and policymaking. Unfortunately, the offices generally are considered not to have achieved this level of impact. Researchers examining the use of oversight and evaluation studies typically have concluded that these products do not have a significant impact on the legislative and policy processes. Beginning in the late 1960s, soon after program evaluation developed as a field, researchers have repeatedly noted that policymakers often do not use the results of evaluation studies. Weiss (1972), writing over thirty years ago, noted that evaluation sponsors often take no action after receiving these reports. Similar findings of lack of policy impact have been reported by numerous other authors.[1] While these negative findings have generally been directed at the evaluation field at large, they are relevant to legislative oversight units. Various authors have reported that legislative use of evaluation studies at the federal level has in fact declined and that legislative oversight is weak and ineffective (Horn, 1995; Chelimsky, 1994; Wargo, 1995).

Part of this depressing assessment is likely due to an overly narrow perspective on what constitutes use of evaluations and oversight studies. Many initial studies of evaluation impact focused on whether the specific recommendations of individual studies were adopted by legislatures and agencies, and these studies generally concluded that such impact did not occur, at least in the short term. However, other authors have argued that there are at least four types of evaluation use (Shulock, 1999; Johnson, 1998; Patton, 1997; Whiteman, 1995):

- Instrumental use, in which recommendations are implemented
- Enlightenment use, in which evaluations influence decision makers' thinking about issues over time

- Process use, in which evaluations promote learning by agencies and other stakeholders who participate in the evaluation
- Symbolic use, in which evaluations are used for political reasons, often to justify decisions already reached about a program

Nonetheless, the widespread criticism of evaluation and oversight studies indicates that the role of oversight offices is often seen as that of a voice crying in the wilderness rather than a key legislative policymaking resource.

Challenges Facing Oversight Offices

Program evaluators and policy analysts face several challenges in achieving use of their work in the legislative process. The studies they produce are intended to provide useful information to elected legislators, who are continually bombarded by massive amounts of information from other sources including lobbyists, other legislative staff, and the media (Arinder, 1997; Whiteman, 1995). The legislative environment is also an oral culture in which personal relationships and anecdotal stories are highly influential (Weiss, 1989; Whiteman, 1995). The pace of legislative decision making is rapid, and the timing of information provision is often essential to its impact on policymaking (Zajano and Lochetfeld, 1999). To have impact, program evaluations and policy analyses must be of high interest to key legislative stakeholders, who must be primed to receive this information. The studies must be convincing enough to break through the noise of competing information yet be readily accessible to policymakers with little time for reading technical reports. The studies must also be timed to meet narrow windows of potential use.

These challenges are complicated because legislative evaluation offices are facing increased competition from other sources of policy research. The offices may have enjoyed a virtual monopoly position as a research provider when they were founded in the 1960s and 1970s, but this is no longer the case. Since that time, there has been a virtual explosion of policy outlets, as hundreds of public and private think tanks have been created that produce studies seeking to influence the policy process (A. Rich, personal communication, Apr. 3, 2006). Furthermore, the political environment in which legislatures operate has undergone major structural changes in recent years. Over the past ten years, a historic shift has occurred in party control of state legislatures. While the majority of state legislatures formerly had been under the control of the Democratic Party for decades, during the late 1990s and early 2000s, the Republican Party captured the majority of state legislative seats and control of legislative chambers for the first time since 1954 (National Conference of State Legislatures, 2004a). Also, term limits took effect in fifteen state legislatures, which forced out many long-standing legislative members (National Conference of State Legislatures, 2004b).

These changes in party control and the substantially increased turnover in legislative seats create a situation of punctuated equilibrium in which existing policy relationships are overturned (Kingdon, 1984; Baumgartner and Jones, 1993). Research has shown that after changes in party control, state legislators in the new majority tend to view existing legislative staff with suspicion and often reduce overall staffing levels (VanLandingham, 2005). For oversight offices, these changes often disrupt long-standing contacts with networks of key legislative stakeholders who understand and support their work.

Strategies to Promote Use

The evaluation utilization literature proposes practical steps that evaluators can take to address these challenges. These steps can be categorized into two overall strategies: (1) establishing strong networks with key legislative stakeholders to identify what information is needed so that their oversight studies can meet these needs and (2) designing and marketing oversight products to promote their ready use within the legislative environment.

Developing Networks for Legislative Stakeholder Access and Input. A great deal of attention has been given in recent years to the importance of network connections among organizations. These networks are critical to information exchange and are particularly important in the legislative environment, as legislators and their staff tend to rely on insider sources close to the process rather than outside information sources (Schneider and others, 2003; Whiteman, 1995; Mooney, 1991; Granovetter, 1973).

Evaluators using this strategy must work to create effective communication channels with key legislative stakeholders to ensure that their oversight products meet the needs of these stakeholders. This often must be a conscious decision by the evaluation office, as it takes time and effort to develop and maintain these network contacts. Time spent developing relationships with legislators and their key staff is time that cannot be spent on other critical tasks, such as carrying out research studies (Schneider and others, 2003).

Stakeholder input should be obtained in all phases of program evaluations and policy analyses (Patton, 1997; Chelimsky, 1994; Sonnichsen, 1994). Thus, evaluators should frequently interact with legislative stakeholders to elicit their ideas and thoughts on these topics:

- What agencies and programs should be studied
- What specific issues should be addressed in the studies
- What research designs should be used (to ensure that the results will be seen as credible)
- How recommendations should be presented (for example, whether legislation is needed to implement the recommendations)
- When report findings and recommendations are needed

It is also important to periodically brief legislators and key staff on research progress in order to promote buy-in and ensure that the studies remain responsive to critical legislative information needs, which may change during the course of the study.

Marketing and Designing User-Friendly Oversight Products. It is also critical that evaluators communicate their research findings to key stakeholders in a manner that is effective in the legislative environment. Evaluators must provide information to distracted stakeholders who receive large volumes of competing information and operate with narrow time windows when decisions must be made. The following steps can be used to communicate effectively in this environment:

• *Produce credible research within short time periods* (Lipton, 1992; Hendricks, 1994; Chelimsky, 1994; Berry, Turcotte, and Latham, 2002). Because many legislative issues arise and must be resolved within short time periods, evaluation offices should have a demonstrated capacity to provide information quickly to meet these needs.

• *Communicate findings in formats that quickly identify key points for busy legislators and key staff* (Carter, 1994; Chelimsky, 1994; Zajano and Lochtefeld, 1999; and Berry, Turcotte, and Latham, 2002). Recommended steps include producing short reports with summaries of key findings; using alternate communication modes such as audiotapes, videotapes, and PowerPoint presentations in addition to written reports; and promoting media coverage of findings through steps such as issuing press releases and holding press conferences.

• *Provide actionable recommendations* (Lipton, 1992; Hendricks, 1994; Sonnichsen, 1994). It is important to recommend actions that are within the legislature's direct control. Although legislators may be interested in recommendations for changes in agency operations, they have a limited capability to mandate administrative details that are within the executive branch's jurisdiction. Program evaluations that make recommendations addressing only internal agency operations, such as modifying procedure manuals or providing additional staff training, are less likely to elicit legislative interest and use. It is also important to provide actionable recommendations in a format that legislators and staff can readily use, such as providing draft bill language and fiscal impact estimates for proposed policy changes.

• *Periodically remind legislators and key staff of nonimplemented prior recommendations* (Carter, 1994; Sonnichsen, 1994; Hendricks, 1994). Evaluators can extend the shelf life of their work by periodically reminding legislative stakeholders of prior findings and recommendations. For example, offices can conduct follow-up studies and publish annual lists of nonimplemented recommendations to bring this information back before legislators when timing may be more suitable for implementation.

Barriers to Utilization Strategies

Although legislative evaluators are "obsessed with utilization" (Jonas, 1999, p. 5), they face barriers to adopting these utilization strategies, including limited time and resources. For example, evaluation offices may lack the staff to conduct follow-up studies in addition to new assignments. The political environment in which the offices operate can also restrict their ability to promote their work, as aggressive marketing can be seen as undue lobbying by staff who are expected to stay in the background.

The professional standards followed by oversight offices may also affect their interactions with their parent state legislators. As Klein (1999) and North (1990) noted, social norms and conventions are part of the institutional environment that shape policy choices. The professional norms of legislative evaluation were laid down in the 1960s and 1970s when most of the offices were created and are highly influenced by their organizational structure. As defined by Berry, Turcotte, and Latham (2002), legislative evaluation offices may be categorized into type 1 units (traditional legislative financial auditing offices that have expanded their work to include program evaluation) and type 2 offices (legislative committees and offices that conduct evaluations as part of their regular work). Both types of offices typically operate relatively independently but under the general oversight of legislative leadership or a joint committee.

Type 1 offices, due to their financial audit work, have generally adopted the Government Auditing Standards promulgated by the U.S. Government Accountability Office.[2] These standards govern the conduct of both financial and performance audits.[3] Some type 2 legislative oversight offices have also adopted the Government Auditing Standards, while others have either not adopted formal standards or follow alternatives such as the Program Evaluation Standards promulgated by the Joint Committee on Standards for Educational Evaluation and the Guiding Principles for Evaluations promulgated by the American Evaluation Association (American Evaluation Association, 2004).

While the prescriptions of these sets of standards are similar, there are important differences that can affect how legislative evaluation offices interact with their parent state legislatures. The most critical of these differences is derived from the Government Auditing Standards Independence standard, which states that "auditors should . . . be sufficiently removed from political pressures to ensure that they can conduct their audits objectively and can report their findings without fear of political repercussion" (U.S. Government Accountability Office, 2003, p. 49). In contrast, the Program Evaluation Standards stress meeting stakeholders' needs: the Utility standard provides that "persons involved in or affected by the evaluation should be identified, so that their needs can be addressed," and "evaluations should be planned, conducted, and reported in ways that encourage follow-through by stakeholders, so that the likelihood that the evaluation will be used is increased" (Joint Committee on Standards for Educational Evaluation, 1994, pp. 25, 59). The Program Evaluation Standards do address potential conflicts of interest in the Propriety standard, which states, "Conflict of interest should be dealt with openly and honestly, so that it does not compromise the evaluation process and results" (p. 115). Similarly, the Guiding Principles state, "Evaluators should negotiate honestly with clients and relevant stakeholders concerning the costs, tasks to be undertaken, limitations of methodology, scope of results likely to be obtained, and uses of data resulting from a specific evaluation. It is primarily the evaluator's responsibility to initiate discussion and clarification of these matters, not the client's" (American Evaluation Association, 2004). Thus, while the Program Evaluation Standards and Guiding Principles encourage offices to disclose conflicts of interest, they also encourage establishing strong network linkages to legislative stakeholders. In contrast, the Government Auditing Standards can discourage this interaction in order to maximize organization independence.

Survey Data

To assess legislative evaluation offices' use of the utilization strategies prescribed by the literature, a survey was conducted of these offices. The primary survey period occurred in spring 2004 and was supplemented by an additional survey effort in spring 2006 when responses were collected from several offices that did not respond to the 2004 survey.[4] The survey was sent to all legislative program evaluation offices that are members of the National Legislative Program Evaluation Society, a staff section of the National Conference of State Legislatures, and responses were received from forty-two of the forty-three offices. The original survey was primarily conducted by e-mail using Perseus software, and the follow-up effort used telephone interviews. In both efforts, the survey asked that a senior manager answer the questions.

Data were gathered by the survey in these areas:

- Organizational status (whether the office fell into the type 1 or type 2 classifications)
- Number of staff allocated to financial auditing versus evaluation activities
- Research standards currently used
- Utilization strategies (whether the office used the networking and marketing steps recommended by the literature)

Data Analysis

The data were used to create three utilization indexes: the first measuring use of the stakeholder network strategies, the second measuring use of the product design and marketing strategies, and the third combining these two. Each index was converted to a standard scale with properties that match the statistical assumptions underlying the *t*-test, a preferred method of analysis. Statistical tests found the indices to be highly reliable.

Results

The analysis found that the organizational design of legislative evaluation offices substantially affects their strategies to pursue use of their work. Specifically, offices that are located within traditional auditing units (type 1) and those that have adopted the Yellow Book standards (that is, the Government Auditing Standards) made significantly lower use of the utilization strategies than offices that report more directly to the legislature and have adopted other research standards (type 2). These findings have implications for evaluators who seek to promote use of their work in other types of settings.

Overall Use of the Utilization Strategies. As shown in Table 2.1, the offices ranged widely in their use of the utilization strategies suggested by the literature, with the widest proportional difference in the use of legislative stakeholder network strategies. One of the most striking findings of the survey was that most offices had relatively low utilization scores. No office used all of the strategies to promote use; the highest score attained by any single office was 83, and the average was 64.95 of the possible 101 points. The average evaluation office had a stakeholder networking score of 27.81 (out of a possible 43), and a product/marketing score of 37.14 (out of a possible 58).

As shown in Table 2.2, about half (twenty) of the offices made relatively high use (attaining two-thirds or more of the possible index points) of the stakeholder networking strategies, while slightly over a third (fifteen, or 36 percent) made high use of the marketing/product design strategies, and eighteen offices made high use of the overall utilization strategies. In contrast, six offices were making low use (under half of the possible index points) of stakeholder networking strategies, one made low use of the product design/marketing strategies, and three made low use of the overall utilization strategies. This pattern indicates that many oversight offices face

Table 2.1. Oversight Offices Varied Substantially in Utilization Strategy Scores

Strategy Category	*Average Score*	*Lowest Score*	*Highest Score*
Networking	27.81	15	41
Marketing	37.14	27	49
Overall	64.95	47	83

Note: $N = 42$. Maximum possible index scores: network, 43; marketing, 58; overall utilization, 101.

Table 2.2. Most Oversight Offices Had Moderate Overall Utilization Strategy Scores

	Number of Offices		
Utilization Scores (Percentage of Possible)	*Networking*	*Marketing*	*Overall*
High (67 percent or higher)	20	15	18
Moderate (50 to 66 percent)	17	26	21
Low (less than 50 percent)	6	1	3

Note: N = 42.

Table 2.3. Oversight Offices Located in Audit Organizations Had Significantly Lower Utilization Strategy Scores Than Offices Located in Legislative Units

Office Type	*Mean z*	*Standard Error*	*t*	*Significance*
Overall Utilization Index				
Auditor ($n = 21$)	−4.0163	2.59750		
Legislative ($n = 21$)	4.0163	2.46607	−2.243	.031
Networking Index				
Auditor ($n = 21$)	−3.1251	1.41534		
Legislative ($n = 21$)	3.1251	1.41879	−3.119	.003
Marketing Index				
Auditor ($n = 21$)	−.8911	1.65045		
Legislative ($n = 21$)	.8911	1.60889	−.773	.444

Note: The mirrored values of z scores in the table are the result of the equal n size in this analysis.

relatively steep challenges in gaining use of their work by their parent state legislatures. This may in part explain the general perception that oversight studies have relatively little impact in the legislative process.

Effect of Organizational Design. The institutional design of legislative oversight offices was highly related to their utilization strategies. As shown in Table 2.3, the type 1 offices located in traditional financial audit organizations had markedly lower stakeholder network, product design and marketing, and overall utilization scores than did the type 2 offices located in legislative committees or units. The table shows the mean z scores of the two types of offices (z scores show deviation and are used to assess differences when items are measured on different scales). The difference in index scores between the two types of offices was statistically significant for both stakeholder networking and overall utilization index scores and empirically supports the concept that an office's normative emphasis on independence is negatively associated with its actions to work with key stakeholders. The marketing efforts of the oversight offices, however, do not appear to vary based on their institutional design. (The subcomponents of the marketing index—legislative marketing, media marketing, alternative products, and supplemental products—also showed no relationship.)

The research norms followed by the evaluation offices were similarly associated with their utilization strategies. As shown in Table 2.4, offices that had adopted the Government Auditing Standards had markedly lower utilization scores than the offices that had not adopted these standards, and the differences in both stakeholder network and overall utilization index scores were statistically significant. Thus, institutional norms (namely the focus on independence) were strongly associated with the offices' behavior in working with legislative stakeholders and actively marketing their evaluation reports.

Conclusion

While legislative oversight offices, like many evaluation and policy analysis units, face substantial challenges in promoting use of their work by policymakers, they often have not taken steps to overcome these challenges by adopting the strategies suggested by the evaluation literature. Although the offices seek utilization, they have not fully heeded the call to deliver utilization-focused evaluations (Patton, 1997) that strategically engage stakeholders and are designed and marketed to promote use by policymakers.

The organizational design and research norms of the offices appear to play a substantial role in constraining their outreach and marketing efforts. Offices that are located in traditional financial auditing units or have adopted traditional auditing standards are apparently often unwilling or unable to form close networks with legislative stakeholders and to promote their work. These offices apparently believe that such activities could pose a threat to their organizational independence.

While this inward focus on independence likely affects legislative use of the evaluations produced by these offices, this impact is difficult to ascertain. It is difficult to measure (or even define) the use of policy research products, particularly in the short term. A needed extension of this study would be to

Table 2.4. Offices That Had Adopted the Government Auditing Standards Had Lower Utilization Strategy Scores

Standards Followed	*Mean z*	*Standard Error*	*t*	*Significance*
Total Utilization Index				
Government Auditing (n = 22)	−4.1507	2.09659		
Other (n = 20)	4.5657	2.91940	−2.458	.018
Networking Index				
Government Auditing (n = 22)	−2.9956	1.31318		
Other (n = 20)	3.3251	1.52671	−3.140	.003
Marketing Index				
Government Auditing (n = 22)	−1.1551	1.30557		
Other (n = 20)	1.2706	1.93001	−1.058	.296

examine the relationship between evaluators' outreach efforts and the familiarity, satisfaction with, and use of their work by policymakers.

Nonetheless, these findings provide insight into policymakers' widely reported limited use of evaluation studies. Simply put, we have met the enemy, and they are often us. Too often evaluators are not doing the things that are necessary to work effectively in today's legislative environment. Evaluators who seek to have their work actively used by government policymakers—and virtually all have this goal regardless of whether they work in the legislative, executive, nonprofit, or private sectors—need to take responsibility for establishing close working relationships with these persons, and actively designing and marketing work products for ready use in the fast-paced policy environment. Evaluators who fail to take these steps likely limit their role to that of a voice crying in the wilderness and forgo the opportunity to effectively speak truth to power.

Notes

1. Patton (1997) provided a depressing summary of negative utilization findings. These included, "The recent literature is unanimous in announcing the general failure of evaluation to affect decision making in a significant way" (Wholey and others, 1970, 46); "[there is] little evidence to indicate that government . . . [has] succeeded in linking social research and decision making" (Cohen and Garet, 1975, 19); "the impact of research on the most important aspects of the state was, with few exceptions, nil" (Deitchman, 1976, 390); and, "It has proved very difficult to uncover many instances where social science research has had a clear and direct impact on policy even when it has been specifically commissioned by government" (Sharpe, 1977, 45).

2. Use of the Government Auditing Standards is mandated by the federal government for audits of programs receiving federal funds. Type 1 organizations review their state's use of federal funds under the Single Audit Act and are thus subject to this mandate.

3. The Government Auditing Standards establish standards in four general areas: Qualifications (needed staff expertise); Independence (the unit and the staff conducting the audit must have both organizational and professional independence from the entity being audited); Due Professional Care, which addresses the procedures to be used in carrying out audit engagements; and Quality Control, addressing documentation and review requirements for audit engagements. The Program Evaluation Standards are categorized into four areas: Utility—the evaluation should address stakeholder needs; Feasibility—the evaluation must be realistic, prudent, diplomatic, and frugal; Propriety—the evaluation must be conducted legally, ethically, and with due regard for the welfare of those involved; and Accuracy—the evaluation will provide technically adequate information.

4. While the 2006 survey occurred in a later time period, the responses can appropriately be aggregated with those collected in 2004, as respondents indicated that their offices had not materially changed their networking and marketing strategies in recent years.

References

American Evaluation Association. *The Guiding Principles for Evaluators.* Fairhaven, Mass.: American Evaluation Association, 2004. Retrieved Dec. 31, 2006, from www.eval.org.

Arinder, M. "Marketing Evaluation Reports." Paper presented to the National Legislative Program Evaluation Society 1997 Training Conference, Jackson, Miss.

Baumgartner, F., and Jones, B. *Agendas and Instability in American Politics.* Chicago: University of Chicago Press, 1993.

Berry, F., Turcotte, J., and Latham, S. "Program Evaluation in State Legislatures: Professional Services Delivered in a Complex, Competitive Environment." In R. Mohan, D. Bernstein, and M. Whitsett (eds.), *Responding to Sponsors and Stakeholders in Complex Environments.* New Directions for Evaluation, no. 95. San Francisco: Jossey-Bass, 2002.

Bezruki, D., Mueller, J., and McKim, K. "Legislative Utilization of Evaluations." In R. K. Jonas (ed.), *Legislative Program Evaluation: Utilization-Driven Research for Decision Makers.* New Directions for Evaluation, no. 81. San Francisco: Jossey-Bass, 1999.

Carter, R. "Maximizing the Use of Evaluation Research." In J. Wholey, H. Hatry, and K. Newcomer (eds.), *Handbook of Practical Program Evaluation.* San Francisco: Jossey-Bass, 1994.

Chelimsky, E. "Making Evaluation Units Effective." In J. Wholey, H. Hatry, and K. Newcomer (eds.), *Handbook of Practical Program Evaluation.* San Francisco: Jossey-Bass, 1994.

Cohen, D., and Garet, M. "Reforming Educational Policy with Applied Social Research." *Harvard Education Review,* 1975, *45,* 67–84.

Deitchman, S. *The Best-Laid Schemes: A Tale of Social Research and Bureaucracy.* Cambridge, Mass.: MIT Press, 1976.

Epstein, D., and O'Halloran, S. "Administrative Procedures, Information, and Agency Discretion." *American Journal of Political Science,* 1994, *38,* 697–722.

Epstein, D., and O'Halloran, S. *Delegating Powers: A Transaction Cost Politics Approach to Policy Making Under Separate Powers.* Cambridge, U.K.: Cambridge University Press, 1999.

Gilligan, T., and Krehbiel, K. "Collective Decision-Making and Standing Committees: An Informal Rationale for Restrictive Amendment Procedures." *Journal of Law, Economics, and Organization,* 1987, *3,* 287–335.

Gilligan, T., and Krehbiel, K. "Collective Choice Without Procedural Commitment." In P. Ordershook (ed.), *Models of Strategic Choice in Politics.* Ann Arbor: University of Michigan Press, 1989.

Granovetter, M. "The Strength of Weak Ties." *American Journal of Sociology,* 1973, *78,* 1360–1380.

Hendricks, M. "Making a Splash: Reporting Evaluation Results Effectively." In J. Wholey, H. Hatry, and K. Newcomer (eds.), *Handbook of Practical Program Evaluation.* San Francisco: Jossey-Bass, 1994.

Horn, M. *The Political Economy of Public Administration: Institutional Choice in the Public Sector.* Cambridge, U.K.: Cambridge University Press, 1995.

Ingraham, P. *The Foundation of Merit: Public Service in American Democracy.* Baltimore, Md.: Johns Hopkins University Press, 1995.

Johnson, R. B. "Toward a Theoretical Model of Evaluation Utilization." *Evaluation and Program Planning,* 1998, *2,* 93–100.

Joint Committee on Standards for Educational Evaluation. *The Program Evaluation Standards.* (2nd ed.) Thousand Oaks, Calif.: Sage, 1994.

Jonas, R. K. "Against the Whim: State Legislatures' Use of Program Evaluation." In R. K. Jonas (ed.), *Legislative Program Evaluation: Utilization-Driven Research for Decision Makers.* New Directions for Evaluation, no. 81. San Francisco: Jossey-Bass, 1999.

Kingdon, J. *Agendas, Alternatives, and Public Policies.* New York: Little, Brown, 1984.

Klein, P. "New Institutional Economics." In B. Bouckeart and G. DeGeest (eds.), *Encyclopedia of Law and Economics.* Cheltenham, U.K.: Edward Elgar and the University of Ghent, 1999.

Knight, J. *Institutions and Social Conflict.* Cambridge, U.K.: Cambridge University Press, 1996.

Lipton, D. S. "How to Maximize Utilization of Evaluation Research by Policymakers." *Annals of the American Academy of Political and Social Science,* 1992, *521,* 175–188.
McCubbins, M., Noll, R., and Weingast, B. "Structure and Process, Politics, and Policy: Administrative Procedures as Instruments of Political Control." *Virginia Law Review,* 1989, *75,* 431–482.
McCubbins, M., and Schwartz, T. "Congressional Oversight Overlooked: Police Patrols Versus Fire Alarms." *American Journal of Political Science,* 1984, *2,* 165–179.
Moe, T. "The Politics of Bureaucratic Structure." In J. Chubb and P. Peterson (eds.), *Can the Government Govern?* Washington, D.C.: Brookings Institution, 1989.
Mooney, C. "Information Sources in State Legislative Decision Making." *Legislative Studies Quarterly,* 1991, *16,* 445–455.
National Conference of State Legislatures. *Program Evaluation in the States.* Denver: National Conference of State Legislatures, 2002.
National Conference of State Legislatures. *State Budget Update.* Denver: National Conference of State Legislatures, 2003.
National Conference of State Legislatures. *Elections Database.* Denver: National Conference of State Legislatures, 2004a.
National Conference of State Legislatures. *Legislative Term Limits: An Overview.* Denver: National Conference of State Legislatures, 2004b.
North, D. *Institutions, Institutional Change and Economic Performance.* Cambridge, U.K.: Cambridge University Press, 1990.
Osborne, D. *Laboratories of Democracy.* Boston: Harvard Business School Press, 1990.
Patton, M. *Utilization-Focused Evaluation: The New Century Text.* (3rd ed.) Thousand Oaks, Calif.: Sage, 1997.
Schneider, M., and others. "Building Consensual Institutions: Networks and the National Estuary Program." *American Journal of Political Science,* 2003, *47,* 143–158.
Sharpe, L. "The Social Scientist and Policymaking: Some Cautionary Thoughts and Transatlantic Reflections." In C. Weiss (ed.), *Using Social Research for Public Policy Making.* Lanham, Md.: Lexington Books, 1977.
Shulock, N. "The Paradox of Policy Analysis: If It Is Not Used, Why Do We Produce So Much of It?" *Journal of Policy Analysis and Management,* 1999, *18,* 226–244.
Sonnichsen, R. "Evaluators as Change Agents." In J. Wholey, H. Hatry, and K. Newcomer (eds.), *Handbook of Practical Program Evaluation.* San Francisco: Jossey-Bass, 1994.
Tubbesing, C. "The State-Federal Tug of War." *State Legislatures,* July–Aug. 1999, pp. 15–21.
U.S. Government Accountability Office. *Government Auditing Standards, 2003 Revision.* Washington, D.C.: Government Accountability Office, 2003.
VanLandingham, G. *Ensuring the Public Trust: How Program Policy Evaluation Serves State Legislatures.* Denver: National Conference of State Legislatures, 2001.
VanLandingham, G. *Ensuring the Public Trust 2004: Program Policy Evaluation's Role in Serving State Legislatures.* Denver: National Conference of State Legislatures, 2004.
VanLandingham, G. "When the Equilibrium Breaks, the Staffing Will Fall—Effects of Changes in Party Control of State Legislatures and Imposition of Term Limits on Legislative Staffing." *Journal of the American Society of Legislative Clerks and Secretaries,* 2005, *11,* 27–42.
Wargo, M. "The Impact of Federal Government Reinvention on Federal Evaluation Activity." *Evaluation Practice,* 1995, *16,* 227–237.
Weiss, C. *Evaluation Action Programs: Readings in Social Action and Education.* Needham Heights, Mass.: Allyn and Bacon, 1972.
Weiss, C. "Congressional Committees as Users of Analysis." *Journal of Policy Analysis and Management,* 1989, *8,* 411–431.
Whiteman, D. *Communication in Congress: Members, Staff, and the Search for Information.* Lawrence: University Press of Kansas, 1995.

Wholey, J., and others. *Federal Evaluation Policy: Analyzing the Effects of Public Programs.* Washington, D.C.: Urban Institute, 1970.
Wildavsky, A. *Speaking Truth to Power: The Art and Craft of Policy Analysis.* New Brunswick, N.J.: Transaction Books, 1979.
Wohlstetter, P. "The Politics of Legislative Evaluations: Fire Alarm and Police Patrol as Oversight Procedures." *Evaluation Practice,* 1990, *11,* 25–32.
Zajano, N., and Lochtefeld, S. "The Nature of Knowledge and Language in the Legislative Arena." In K. Jonas (ed.), *Legislative Program Evaluation: Utilization-Driven Research for Decision Makers.* New Directions for Evaluation, no. 81. San Francisco: Jossey-Bass, 1999.

GARY R. VANLANDINGHAM is director of the Florida legislature's Office of Program Policy Analysis and Government Accountability.

3

Whether a study will have legislative impact often depends on multiple factors that may be beyond the control of evaluators. Nevertheless, evaluators can play an important role in facilitating the convergence of factors that can create legislative impact.

Evaluators' Role in Facilitating the Convergence of Factors to Create Legislative Impact

Hal Greer

In 1999, the staff of the Joint Legislative Audit and Review Commission (JLARC) of the Virginia General Assembly (the state legislature) completed a review of the Virginia Board of Medicine that found problems with the process used to regulate physicians and recommended major changes to a system that had remained relatively unchanged for almost seventy years (Virginia, 1999). JLARC is an oversight agency of the Virginia General Assembly and comprises fourteen senior legislators as well as a nonpartisan staff of legislative evaluators who conduct independent policy studies requested by the legislators. While legislative political factors that were not disclosed to the evaluators might have contributed to the legislative action taken in response to the study, evaluators played a key role in facilitating the convergence of factors that led to legislative reform.

Evaluators contributed to this convergence through the use of four strategies: (1) establishment of report credibility through the research process, (2) development of a report that effectively conveyed study findings, (3) establishment of a professional working relationship with the press, and (4) provision of necessary support and assistance to policymakers. All of these strategies contributed to the legislative impact that resulted from the evaluation of the Board of Medicine's disciplinary process.

WILEY InterScience®
DISCOVER SOMETHING GREAT

NEW DIRECTIONS FOR EVALUATION, no. 112, Winter 2006 © Wiley Periodicals, Inc.
Published online in Wiley InterScience (www.interscience.wiley.com) • DOI: 10.1002/ev.206

Overview of Board of Medicine Study and Legislative Action

One of the most secretive regulatory programs in Virginia government historically has been the process of regulating the practice of medicine through a system established to discipline physicians for misconduct or substandard practice. The Board of Medicine, which comprises primarily physicians, administers this system. Under Virginia law, individuals may file complaints with the board alleging misconduct by a physician who has treated them. Board staff investigate the complaints, and the board decides whether to proceed to a hearing based on probable cause or to close the case. At the time of the study, most cases were closed administratively with a determination that probable cause was not established. The majority of cases that proceeded to a hearing were resolved through informal conferences that were closed to the public.

Representatives of several groups, including the Virginia Hospital and Healthcare Association and the Virginia Association of Health Plans, were concerned that the board was not adequately policing the medical practice. Most of the cases were being closed without a hearing, and only a few physicians were sanctioned by the board. In addition, there were concerns about the accountability of the board given the secret nature of the process and the system's reliance on physicians to regulate their own.

JLARC Study of the Board of Medicine. As a result of these concerns, the 1998 General Assembly requested JLARC to study the effectiveness of this regulatory process. During the following year, JLARC staff conducted a comprehensive review of Virginia's health regulatory boards with the primary focus on the Board of Medicine. The review included an examination of more than two hundred disciplinary cases resolved by the board, as well as interviews with board members and staff, investigative staff, attorneys who appeared before the board, and others involved in the process (Virginia, 1999).

The study found that the board was not adequately disciplining physicians and was failing to adequately protect the public. The JLARC report included recommendations to address the report findings. The most significant finding was that the Board of Medicine was rarely taking action to sanction physicians for standard-of-care violations. Most of the sanctions that were imposed by the board were for substance abuse or sexual misconduct. Only 3 percent of the cases in which violations were found by the Board of Medicine in the 1997 and 1998 fiscal years were based on substandard care. This was in sharp contrast to other boards that regulated health professions. For example, 64 percent of the sanctions imposed by the Board of Pharmacy and 28 percent of the sanctions imposed by the Board of Nursing involved standard-of-care violations during the same time period (Virginia, 1999).

One of the primary conclusions of the report was that the lack of standard-of-care violations found by the board appeared to be related to the statutory criterion used to assess whether a violation had occurred. Since 1932, the Code of Virginia had stipulated that disciplinary action could be taken against physicians only if their conduct constituted gross negligence unless they posed a danger to the health and welfare of their patients or the public. The study found that with this high threshold for deciding standard-of-care cases, physicians were rarely held accountable for providing poor care unless there was evidence of an egregious act or pattern of acts of negligence. The review also found that no other health regulatory board in Virginia had such a high threshold for deciding standard of care cases. In addition, the Federation of State Medical Boards recommended a negligence criterion that constituted a lower threshold than the "gross negligence" one used by the Virginia Board of Medicine.

Based on these findings, the report recommended that the Code of Virginia be amended to lower the threshold for what conduct would constitute a violation of law. Instead of requiring the board to find that a physician had been grossly negligent in the practice of medicine in order to discipline him or her, the board would have to find only that the physician had acted negligently (Virginia, 1999). For example, prior to this statutory change, a physician who killed his thirteen-year-old patient by mistakenly perforating her artery during the insertion of a catheter was determined by the Board of Medicine not to have been grossly negligent and therefore was not disciplined. With the new negligence threshold, this physician likely would have been found to have acted negligently and therefore subjected to disciplinary action.

There were two other major findings from the review. The analysis revealed that delays in processing serious cases could threaten public safety. Cases that ultimately resulted in the suspension or revocation of a physician's license were taking more than three years to resolve on average, and physicians continued to be able to practice without restriction until the case was resolved. Through the JLARC review, it was also determined that some cases were being dismissed at the intake stage without a full investigation of the allegations submitted to the board. The report included recommendations to address these two findings (Virginia, 1999).

Reaction to the Study. Staff presented the findings of the report to JLARC in June 1999. A strong reaction immediately followed the staff's presentation of the study findings. One legislator commented that it was the most devastating report in his twenty-five years serving on the JLARC commission (King, 1999). Several newspapers published headline stories that highlighted the study findings. Nevertheless, despite this initial reaction, no action was taken by the General Assembly over the next three years to address the major recommendations in the report.

One of the primary reasons that the General Assembly appeared to take no action despite its strong reaction to the report findings was the influence of the Medical Society of Virginia. The society, which represents physicians and actively lobbies the General Assembly on their behalf, opposed most of the study recommendations.

Newspaper Investigation. Then in the spring of 2002, a reporter for a major Virginia newspaper began investigating a story that a physician had harmed multiple patients over an eleven-year period during which the Board of Medicine did not act to revoke his license. In conducting the investigation, the reporter contacted legislative evaluators to discuss the board's disciplinary process. The reporter also consulted with evaluators regarding the study findings and recommendations as they related to the story that she was pursuing. On June 23, 2002, three years after the JLARC study findings were presented publicly, the newspaper published a series of articles that documented the misconduct of this physician and the lack of action taken by the Board of Medicine to discipline him. Along with the series of articles about this specific physician and his patients, the newspaper published an article detailing the findings from the 1999 JLARC study (Szabo, 2002a, 2002b).

Proposal for Reform. A freshman legislator who read the newspaper series was disturbed by the study findings and concerned to discover that the General Assembly had taken no action following the JLARC report. At the legislator's request, legislative evaluators met with her to discuss the JLARC study findings in more detail. She then requested evaluators to draft legislation that would lower the legal criterion from gross to simple negligence in standard-of-care cases, as well as implement other study recommendations.

After the draft legislation was developed, this legislator met with the interested parties during the fall of 2002 about the proposed legislation, in hopes of addressing their concerns and gaining their support for it. Initially there was strong resistance to the proposed legislation from the Medical Society of Virginia. A lobbyist for the society downplayed the seriousness of the report findings and asserted that the Board of Medicine had ample authority under existing law to discipline physicians. He also claimed that the proposed legislation was unnecessary and that the proposed changes would not improve the process (Szabo, 2002b). However, this freshman legislator, with the assistance of legislative evaluators, effectively countered these assertions through the use of case examples, quantitative analysis, and other detailed findings presented in the JLARC report. Eventually the medical society became less interested in resisting the legislation and more focused on working with the legislator to make the legislation more acceptable to the physicians it represented.

Legislative Action. After meetings were held through the fall with the Medical Society of Virginia, the Virginia Hospital and Healthcare Association, the Department of Health Professions, and the Board of Medicine, consensus was reached regarding the proposed legislation, and all of the stakeholders agreed to support it during the legislative session. In addition, the legislator met with the leadership from both parties in the House and

Senate to update party leaders on her progress in developing the proposed legislation and to gain their support for it. JLARC continued to provide support to the legislator in meetings with the Medical Society, Hospital Association, and Board of Medicine to discuss technical aspects of the legislation, but did not take part in meetings among legislators in which the proposed legislation was discussed in the context of political strategy. This support consisted of serving as an informational resource as questions arose and amending the proposed legislation to address concerns of the various stakeholders.

By the start of the 2003 legislative session, the proposed legislation had the support of the various stakeholders, including the Medical Society of Virginia, as well as most legislators in both houses of the General Assembly. The introduced legislation was passed with overwhelming majorities in both the House and the Senate and signed into law by the governor. The result was the enactment of legislation during the 2003 Virginia General Assembly session that implemented many of the recommendations in the JLARC report. The legislation placed substantially greater responsibility on the Board of Medicine to protect the public by requiring the board to sanction physicians who act negligently in providing substandard care, fully investigate all reports or complaints against physicians, and regularly report on case processing times.

Convergence of Factors

While the convergence of factors that led to legislative impact was to some extent beyond the control of legislative evaluators, the use of utilization strategies and the presence of some elements within their control increased the possibility of this type of convergence.

Establishing Report Credibility. One of the strategies that the legislative evaluators used was the establishment of report credibility through the research process. Establishing credibility was especially important in this instance given the subject of the study and the political dynamics. There was strong resistance to the study within the medical community. The general view held by physicians was that it was not appropriate or necessary to review their well-established disciplinary process, and legislative evaluators who lacked medical training were not qualified to conduct such a review.

As a result of these factors, establishing credibility through the research design was a priority for JLARC evaluators. Evaluators met with or surveyed most of the key participants in the disciplinary system to gain their perspective and build credibility with them. Interviews were conducted with most of the members of the Board of Medicine as well as several past members, the board staff, and attorneys who represented physicians before the board. Along with these interviews, current and former board members were surveyed to elicit their ideas and thoughts about the disciplinary process.

In addition to the interviews and board survey, extensive data collection was undertaken to fully understand the board's disciplinary process, accurately identify the relevant issues, and adequately support the study findings. More than two hundred disciplinary cases were reviewed in detail. For each case, the complete board file was examined. In addition, JLARC staff attended numerous disciplinary proceedings of the Board of Medicine that were conducted during the study period.

One of the biggest challenges was how to establish credibility in making judgments about cases before the board given that none of the legislative evaluators were medical experts. A key finding of the study was that the board was not taking action against physicians in cases that involved negligent conduct. To support this finding, the study team had to make judgments about whether the alleged misconduct by physicians in the cases before the board constituted negligent care. The approach taken was to identify cases that appeared to involve negligence in the practice of medicine and then to have Board of Medicine staff review the cases with evaluators and confirm that the alleged misconduct constituted negligent or substandard care. Cases that could not be confirmed as negligent care cases were not used in the report as case examples. This approach provided additional support for the study's findings and increased the overall credibility of the report.

Study Findings. A second utilization strategy used was the development of a written report that conveyed compelling study findings in a way that was easily understandable, clearly identified the problem and the needed solution, and presented a convincing case that action was needed to address it. One of the key ways this strategy was implemented in the study was through the use of powerful case examples obtained from file reviews.

The most significant finding from the study was that the Board of Medicine was not taking action against physicians who were negligent in the practice of medicine. Legislative evaluators determined that the best way to convey the seriousness of the finding and the need for legislative action was through case examples. Evaluators developed a template for constructing each example. An example of a case presented in the report follows:

> A physician allegedly provided substandard care in the performance of surgery for vertigo, an illusory sense that the environment or one's own body is revolving. The surgery resulted in partial facial paralysis of the patient. The paralysis allegedly resulted from damage to the patient's facial nerve by the physician. The complaint was received by the Board of Medicine as a medical malpractice payment report. The report indicated that there was a verdict in favor of the plaintiff. The malpractice suit was ultimately settled for $601,800. The disciplinary case was closed by the Board without a hearing [Virginia General Assembly, 1999, p. 75].

The goal was to communicate the seriousness of the misconduct and the resulting consequences concisely and in a way that was easily understandable.

Each case example succinctly described the physician's mistake, the harm to the patient that resulted from the negligent act, the nature of the complaint, and how the board handled it. Through the examples, legislative evaluators were able to convey effectively the gravity of the allegations against physicians in the cases before the board and the degree to which the board's inaction threatened public safety.

In addition to the use of case examples to identify the problem and present a compelling case for action, legislative evaluators developed a specific solution to address it. The report included a recommendation that referenced the section of the Code of Virginia that needed to be amended and specifically described the need to change the gross negligence criterion and define the negligent practice of medicine as a violation of law. This change was significant because the gross negligence standard was ambiguous, and members of the board, who were reluctant to take action against their peers for substandard practice, had construed the standard as requiring a pattern of substandard care. However, there was no guidance as to how many incidents of substandard care were required to meet this threshold, and it was difficult to establish a pattern because of the board's reluctance to take action regarding individual incidents of substandard care. The ambiguity of the standard and the wide discretion it afforded the board were eliminated by amending the statute to specify that a negligent act would be considered a violation of law.

Legislative evaluators provided support for the recommendation by comparing and contrasting the criterion that other health regulatory boards used. The report noted that the other nine Virginia boards that regulate licensees who provide direct health care to patients all use a negligence criterion and that boards of medicine in neighboring states apply a negligence criterion as well. The report also discussed the recommendation of the Federation of State Medical Boards, a national organization that provides policy guidance to state medical boards, that medical boards take disciplinary action against licensees for the "negligent" practice of medicine.

Establishing a Professional Working Relationship with the Press. Two additional elements that were in the control of evaluators after the release of the report enhanced the possibility of its use. The first was the establishment of a professional working relationship with the press that included being accessible and providing the media with the factual information needed to understand the issues and prepare news articles that accurately conveyed study findings.

JLARC's director regularly emphasizes the important role that the media can play in publicizing the findings of the agency's evaluation work and the need to be a useful and responsive resource, so that reporters can understand study findings and place them in proper context. Legislative evaluators also have been counseled on the importance of providing factual information to the media and the basis or rationale for study findings but to avoid offering opinions. As a result of this relationship, the newsprint media in Virginia tend to rely on studies and information provided by legislative evaluators regarding the subject areas with which JLARC has experience and expertise and tend to present JLARC study findings to the extent they are relevant to the issue being covered.

In this instance, the investigative reporter pursuing the story of the physician contacted JLARC staff to discuss the Board of Medicine and its disciplinary process. Legislative evaluators were then able to provide background information on the disciplinary process and share with the reporter the significance and relevance of its study of the board in the context of the issues on which the press was reporting. This led to the newspaper's decision to feature the JLARC study as part of its series of articles on the physician. Publishing an article on the JLARC study, along with the series on the physician, was the critical link that prompted the freshman legislator, who had not been serving in the General Assembly at the time the report was originally released, to make the connection and contact JLARC staff for assistance in developing proposed legislation to address the concerns highlighted in the articles.

Providing Needed Support and Assistance. The other element present was legislative evaluators who were ready and available to provide support and assistance to legislators as needed when the opportunity for this type of convergence arose, so that legislators could successfully navigate the challenges associated with proposing major legislative change. There was strong opposition to the legislative changes that were proposed initially. In an effort to dissuade the freshman legislator from pursuing the proposed legislative reform, the Medical Society asserted that its system was adequate and that the proposed changes would not improve the disciplinary process.

This freshman legislator, who was new to the legislative process and serving in a part-time legislature, did not have any policy experience in the health care area or the regulation of health care professionals and had no policy staff. Therefore, she was at a significant disadvantage in dealing with the Medical Society, which had its own policy experts. To maintain her momentum and keep the proposed reform viable, she needed to be able to respond effectively to and address the contentions of the Medical Society. She called on legislative evaluators, who made themselves available to serve as this support. They drafted the proposed legislation and played a critical role in responding to the assertions and arguments of the Medical Society. She requested that these evaluators accompany her to all of the meetings with stakeholders, and she asked the evaluators to engage in the debate with the Medical Society and respond to all of its contentions. In this instance, evaluators played a key role in helping her address the concerns and objections raised by opponents of the proposed legislation and proposing solutions to address them.

One of the major challenges for legislative evaluators through this active involvement in the process was to manage the politics of the situation effectively. This was essential to maintain the credibility of the report findings and recommendations. Evaluators therefore remained focused on providing accurate, relevant, and reliable information based on the study findings. They were careful not to offer opinions other than recommendations presented in the report, and they declined to participate in the political strategy sessions between the freshman legislator and her party leadership regarding the proposed legislation.

Conclusion

While the legislative impact of program evaluations is subject to the decisions and actions of policymakers, this case example demonstrates that legislative evaluators and their studies can play a key role in influencing the policymaking process. Legislators' decisions resulting from political strategies are beyond evaluators' control, but in this instance, the strategies and actions of legislative evaluators contributed to the convergence of factors that ultimately led to significant legislative action. A research design that established credibility and a report that conveyed the findings in a compelling and easily understandable way ensured that the report would be noticed, understood, and seriously considered by policymakers and the media. In addition, legislative evaluators' relationship with the press, as well as the continued support and assistance provided to legislators as the legislation was drafted, also were essential to the convergence of factors that led to legislative action.

References

King, L. "Study: State Slow to Investigate Doctors." *Virginian-Pilot,* June 15, 1999, p. A1.
Szabo, L. "Operating Behind Closed Doors." *Virginian-Pilot,* June 23, 2002a, p. A1.
Szabo, L. "Warnings Have Gone Unheeded." *Virginian-Pilot,* June 23, 2002b, p. A14.
Virginia General Assembly. Joint Legislative Audit and Review Commission. *Final Report: Review of Health Regulatory Boards.* Richmond: Commonwealth of Virginia, Aug. 1999.

HAL GREER is division chief at the Joint Legislative Audit and Review Commission of the Virginia General Assembly.

4

This chapter describes conditions and strategies that played a role in affecting actions taken by the Florida legislature and the South Carolina General Assembly in their respective Medicaid programs.

The Influence of Evaluators on State Medicaid Policies: Florida and South Carolina's Experience

Yvonne Bigos, Jennifer Johnson, Rae Hendlin, Steve Harkreader, Andrea Truitt

Legislative evaluators can inform state policymakers who face policy and budget decisions related to large and complex federal programs such as Medicaid. Unlike lobbyists, advocates, and other stakeholders who support particular interests, legislative evaluators are uniquely positioned to provide independent and timely information to assist policymakers (Berry, Turcotte, and Latham, 2002). Failing to accurately focus an evaluation toward meeting policymakers' concerns will result in reports that are of little use in policy development (Bezruki, Mueller, and McKim, 1999). This chapter discusses four conditions related to evaluation use, as well as several strategies used by Florida and South Carolina legislative evaluators that facilitated utilization of their Medicaid studies.

Between 2001 and 2006, the Florida Legislature's Office of Program Policy Analysis and Government Accountability (OPPAGA) and the South Carolina Legislative Audit Council (LAC) influenced legislative policy and budget decisions related to Medicaid, a federal program that requires a substantial state contribution. Medicaid programs provide health care services to low-income persons whose health care needs otherwise would not be met. As health care costs have escalated, the proportion of each state's budget spent on Medicaid has grown. In an effort to continue current benefit levels while containing costs, state legislative bodies have focused on this program.

NEW DIRECTIONS FOR EVALUATION, no. 112, Winter 2006 © Wiley Periodicals, Inc.
Published online in Wiley InterScience (www.interscience.wiley.com) • DOI: 10.1002/ev.207

Conditions and Strategies Affecting Evaluation Use

Kingdon (1995) postulated that policy development at the federal level occurs when three streams—the problem stream, the policy stream, and the political stream—converge to open a policy window, an opportunity for policy formation. Kingdon describes these streams as broad, involving participants both inside and outside government and at times as being entrepreneurial and random. While these same broad processes or streams influence policymaking at the state level, the role of evaluators within these processes is more narrowly defined and predictable. Based on Kingdon's model and our observations and experience working within the legislative environment, we recognize four conditions as influencing whether legislative policymakers use evaluations: problem definition, policy alternatives, political environment, and timing. In this section, we describe these four conditions and offer some of the utilization strategies discussed in Chapter Two of this volume that OPPAGA and LAC evaluators employed to facilitate the use of their evaluations by legislators.

Problem Definition. When an issue, event, or question becomes a priority for policymakers, state legislatures can request their legislative evaluation offices to conduct an evaluation and develop policy recommendations for addressing it. While evaluators have little control in establishing that a problem or issue exists, they can verify its significance and shape the scope of an evaluation. By assisting in this process, evaluators can better ensure their reports will be used.

To ensure that evaluations are reasonable and meet legislative needs, OPPAGA and LAC routinely meet with legislative committee staff and legislators to refine, refocus, and clarify evaluation requests. This is especially important when initial requests are unclear, too broad, or not feasible, such as when the legislatures in Florida and South Carolina directed OPPAGA and LAC to "review Medicaid." To be effective in shaping the scope of their studies, evaluators must understand and respond to the needs of their sponsors and stakeholders (Mohan, Bernstein, and Whitsett, 2002; Patton, 1997). They need to be aware of and consider current issues and trends at the national, state, and local levels that are related to the policy issues and problems. For example, LAC evaluators met with legislators and their staff and found that the legislative interest was to reduce Medicaid program costs without reducing services. Similarly, OPPAGA evaluators met with legislative staff to narrow the review of their study of Medicaid. They learned that the legislature was interested in four issues: prescription drug costs, disease management, efforts to control provider fraud and abuse, and the success of prior cost-reduction initiatives. Once OPPAGA and LAC evaluators had determined evaluation scope, they followed up with the appropriate committee staff and legislators to explain changes made to evaluation requests and establish deadlines.

Policy Alternatives. To be useful, evaluators must develop realistic and feasible policy alternatives (Patton, 1997; Grob, 2004). Our experience suggests that legislators are generally cautious and are interested in recommendations that are likely to be cost neutral or capable of producing savings and will maintain or increase access to needed services. In addition, they are more likely to adopt incremental changes, preferring policy recommendations that reflect emerging trends in states or the private sector and where the likely impact of implementing a policy alternative is clear and predictable.

To ensure that policy recommendations are feasible, OPPAGA and LAC consider multiple sources of information, including stakeholder interviews, available data, and related literature. In addition, they assess which strategies will best address problems identified through the evaluation by considering issues such as national trends and feasibility of implementation. It is important for evaluators to describe both positive and negative consequences of policy alternatives, so that policymakers can assess the relative merits, feasibility, costs, or impact any policy change might have. For example, when recommending changes to slow the growth in the cost of long-term care, LAC recognized the nursing home industry's concerns about losing funds that would be shifted to those providing services to patients in their homes and community-based centers. To address this concern, the January 2003 LAC report included a suggestion that nursing homes could be certified to provide home and community-based services.

Political Environment. Although evaluators must consider the political environment in which policymakers will make decisions when developing policy recommendations, they have little direct control over this condition (Palumbo, 1987). In Chapter One of this volume, Mohan and Sullivan describe evaluation as intrinsically political and suggest approaches to managing the politics of evaluation. Support for change is greatest when there is broad consensus that a problem exists. In contrast, a divisive or unfocused political environment may preclude policymakers from considering even well-developed and viable options. Partisanship, competing agendas, or interest from only a few legislators reduces the chance that evaluation results will be used.

Even when the political environment may not support immediate change, evaluators can inform the policymaking process. Over time the political landscape may change, making previous policy recommendations more attractive to legislators. For example, OPPAGA's 2003 pharmacy report recommended requiring that pharmaceutical manufacturers pay supplemental cash rebates for all of their prescription drugs that are included on the state Medicaid preferred-drug list. At the time, the legislature did not use this recommendation and instead continued to exempt behavioral health drugs from the rebate requirement because of pressure by behavioral health advocates. However, despite continued pressure, the legislature adopted this recommendation in 2005 and now requires drug manufacturers to pay supplemental cash rebates for behavioral health drugs.

Timing. Evaluators need to ensure that the right information is available to policymakers at the right time (Berry, Turcotte, and Latham, 2002). Kingdon (1995) argued that a policy window opens to allow change when a focusing event occurs, sound policy alternatives are available, and the political environment is supportive. In Chapter Three of this volume, Greer describes a focusing event in the form of newspaper coverage of physician misconduct three years after legislative evaluators released a report on a consistent lack of disciplinary action by Virginia's Board of Medicine. The report's policy recommendations and a period of intense media attention helped create a political environment conducive to change. The opening of this policy window resulted in statutory changes recommended by legislative evaluators.

Since policy windows may be short-lived, timing is essential. No matter how thorough the evaluation or how feasible the recommendations, a report that misses the policy window will also miss the opportunity to assist the decision-making process. For evaluations to be used in policymaking, evaluators must facilitate the use of their work by taking steps to ensure that legislators have the necessary information when they must make decisions.

OPPAGA and LAC routinely take steps to ensure that legislators and committee staff have necessary information with adequate time for them to understand the issues and alternatives, draft legislation or budget language, and negotiate the political consensus needed to implement the policy recommendations. While succinct, message-driven reports are fundamental for communicating policy recommendations, other efforts to share evaluation results often precede the report's release and allow legislative staff and legislators the opportunity to begin efforts to affect policy change. OPPAGA and LAC meet with legislators and committee staff to discuss results and address questions. When requested, OPPAGA and LAC staff also provide presentations to legislative committees.

Influencing State Medicaid Policy

This section describes how the conditions and strategies discussed influenced the use of legislative evaluations by Florida and South Carolina legislatures to address specific Medicaid issues. Through a series of reviews, both OPPAGA and LAC evaluated critical components of their Medicaid programs, including efforts to contain the costs of Medicaid prescription drugs and to control fraud and abuse by Medicaid recipients and providers. OPPAGA also reviewed Florida's Medicaid disease management initiative, the state's regulation of wholesale drug market practices to prevent counterfeit and diverted drugs, and Florida's hospice services. LAC has assessed South Carolina's process and criteria for determining eligibility for Medicaid services. (See Table 4.1 for a full listing of OPPAGA and LAC Medicaid reports published between 2001 and 2006, their general recommendations, and subsequent legislative actions.)

Table 4.1. Medicaid Reports Published by OPPAGA and LAC, 2001–2006

Issue	*Recommendations and Policy Discussion*	*Reports*	*Type of Use and Action*
Pharmacy: Prescription drug costs (Florida)	OPPAGA recommended the state develop a preferred drug list (PDL), require manufacturers to pay supplemental cash rebates, eliminate value-added contracts with drug manufacturers, modify pharmacy reimbursement formulas, expand state maximum pricing for generic drugs, and negotiate generic drug supplemental rebates.	*Growth in Medicaid Prescription Drug Costs Indicates Additional Prudent Purchasing Practices Are Needed* (Feb. 2001)	Law enacted to develop and implement a PDL. Budget reduced by $213 million in anticipation of savings from PDL.[a]
		Changes to Medicaid Preferred Drug List Requirements and Competitive Bidding Pharmacy Contracts Could Save an Additional $86.6 Million in 2003–04 (Apr. 2003)	Law amended to eliminate option for pharmaceutical companies to provide services with anticipated savings (such as disease management) in lieu of paying supplemental cash rebates.
		Medicaid Disease Management Initiative Has Not Yet Met Cost-Savings and Health Outcomes Expectations (May 2004)	Law amended to add mental health drugs, a previously exempt therapeutic category, to the preferred drug list. Budget reduced by $85.2 million in fiscal year 2004–05 and by $290 million in fiscal year 2006-07 from anticipated savings.
		Inflated Pricing and Confidential Information Prevent Medicaid from Ensuring Lowest Prescription Drug Price (Jan. 2006)	Budget reduced in anticipation of $6.1 million savings by expanding the number of generic drugs subject to state maximum pricing. Debate took place on recommendation to increase the discount

(continued)

Table 4.1. *Continued*

Issue	*Recommendations and Policy Discussion*	*Reports*	*Type of Use and Action*
			off the average wholesale price (AWP) from 15.4 percent to 18 percent. Issue was withdrawn due to pressure from pharmacies.
Pharmacy: Prescription drug costs (South Carolina)	LAC recommended the state implement a PDL, increase use of prior authorization for nonpreferred drugs, and implement drug use policies.	*A Review of Selected Medicaid Issues* (Feb. 2001)	Budget included a proviso that would have implemented recommendations related to prescription drug program changes with a corresponding $4.7 million in funding reductions but failed to pass in the senate.
		Options for Medicaid Cost Containment (Jan. 2003)	Budget required state agency to implement PDL and prior approval for drugs not on that list.
Program integrity: Provider error, abuse, and fraud and drug safety (Florida)	OPPAGA recommended that to reduce provider billing errors, abuse, and fraud, the state should implement stronger prevention, detection, deterrence, and recovery efforts. OPPAGA also recommended ways to improve the safety of prescription medications.	*Medicaid Program Integrity Efforts Recover Minimal Dollars, Sanctions Rarely Imposed, Stronger Accountability Needed* (Sept. 2001)	Senate Select Committee formed to focus on Medicaid fraud and abuse, which resulted in amending law to strengthen agency accountability, specifically increasing provider penalties and agency enforcement authority, and requiring the agency to conduct a payment error study.

		AHCA Takes Steps to Improve Medicaid Program Integrity, But Further Actions Are Needed (Nov. 2004)	Law mandated biennial OPPAGA reviews after presentation of preliminary findings to Senate Health Care Committee in spring 2004 prior to report release.
		Enhanced Detection and Stronger Use of Sanctions Could Improve AHCA's Ability to Detect and Deter Overpayments to Providers (Mar. 2006)	No legislative action.[b]
		Counterfeit and Diverted Drugs Threaten Public Health and Waste State Dollars (Feb. 2003)	Law amended to address pedigree papers, increase criminal penalties, and strengthen wholesaler permit requirements. Fiscal analysis developed by legislative staff used the report to document need to track pedigree papers.[c]
		Legislature Strengthens Pedigree Paper, Wholesaler Permit Requirements to Better Ensure Safe Prescription Drugs[c] (Oct. 2005)	Law strengthened pedigree paper requirements.
Program integrity: Provider and recipient fraud (South Carolina)	LAC recommended the state improve access to and use of interagency and claims data in order to reduce Medicaid recipient and provider fraud.	*A Review of Selected Medicaid Issues* (Feb. 2001)	Budget allowed Medicaid agency to retain collections resulting from expanded program integrity efforts that maximize ability to detect and eliminate provider fraud.
Program administration: Eligibility Determination (South Carolina)	LAC recommended changing application eligibility criteria, renewal periods, length of	*Options for Medicaid Cost Containment* (Jan. 2003)	Debate took place on increasing the cigarette tax to generate needed revenues to act on report findings.

(continued)

Table 4.1. *Continued*

Issue	*Recommendations and Policy Discussion*	*Reports*	*Type of Use and Action*
	transitional Medicaid, and supporting recipients' transfer to alternative insurance. Also recommended changes in staffing and contracting practices in the area of eligibility determination to improve program accountability.	*Cost Saving Strategies for the South Carolina Medicaid Program* (Oct. 2001)	Budget amendment requiring Medicaid agency to assume responsibility for eligibility determination and improve accuracy and integrity of program.
Program administration: Local field offices (Florida)	OPPAGA recommended the state recredential MediPass providers less frequently, develop strategies to reduce the number of problematic Medicaid claims that are manually reviewed, and clarify field office roles.	*Medicaid Field Offices Can Improve Efficiency and Effectiveness; State Could Outsource Some Activities* (May 2004)	No legislative action.[b]
Optional services: Costs and benefits (Florida)	OPPAGA provided information on the costs and benefits of continuing or restoring funding for optional Medicaid services or services to optional populations.	*Continuing Certain Medicaid Options Will Increase Costs, But Benefit Recipients and the State* (Jan. 2005)	Funding continued to provide prenatal care for pregnant women with incomes between 150 and 185 percent of the federal poverty limit; was restored to provide dentures for adults; and continued to provide all needed health services for medically needy individuals.
Hospice services: Regulation and quality (Florida)	OPPAGA recommended that if the legislature allowed programs to operate as for-profit entities, it should continue regulating hospice services through a Certificate of Need process.	*Florida's Certificate of Need Process Ensures Qualified Hospice Programs; Performance Reporting Is Important to Assess Hospice Quality* (Mar. 2006)	Law enacted that allows hospice services to be delivered by for-profit entities, requires hospices to report outcome and quality information, and requires

	OPPAGA also recommended that the legislature require hospice programs to develop standardized quality and outcome measures and a mechanism for collecting and maintaining this information.		OPPAGA to analyze the impact of for-profit hospices on the delivery of care to terminally ill patients.
Funding: Supplemental physician payment (Florida)	OPPAGA assessed the pros and cons of a plan to increase federal Medicaid funds with upper payment limit while reducing general revenue funds.	*Uncertainty Exists Regarding Florida's Proposed Physician Upper Payment Limit Program* (Feb. 2003)	No changes to funding to prevent an increased reliance on upper payment limit to generate more federal funds.
Long-term care: Nursing home diversion (Florida)	OPPAGA described recipient characteristics and differences in services used and assessed the effectiveness of the program in delaying nursing home placement.	*Service Use for Nursing Home Diversion Waiver Clients Depends on Living Situation* (Feb. 2006)	No legislative action.[b]
		The Nursing Home Diversion Program Has Successfully Delayed Nursing Home Entry (May 2006)	No legislative action.[b]
Long-term care: Nursing home use (South Carolina)	LAC recommended the General Assembly consider adding home and community-based care slots, freezing the number of nursing home beds, and changing budget line to give the agency more flexibility to shift funds between these services. It also directed the agency to take steps that would improve access and patient transition between these service locations.	*Options for Medicaid Cost Containment* (Jan. 2003)	No legislative action.[b]

(continued)

Table 4.1. *Continued*

Issue	*Recommendations and Policy Discussion*	*Reports*	*Type of Use and Action*
Disease management: Chronic disease initiative (Florida)	OPPAGA recommended the state redesign the initiative, establish a defensible methodology to assess cost savings, and report on progress in meeting initiative goals and expectations. In a subsequent report, OPPAGA recommended the state remove risk-based expectations from vendor contracts and establish clear performance expectations, assess and report on long-term health outcomes, improve monitoring, and develop strategies to increase Medicaid provider participation.	*Medicaid Disease Management Initiative Sluggish, Cost Savings Not Determined, Design Changes Needed* (May 2001)	No legislative action.[b]
		Medicaid Disease Management Initiative Has Not Yet Met Cost-Savings and Health Outcomes Expectations (May 2004)	No legislative action for disease management but report was used to justify eliminating option for drug companies to provide disease management with guaranteed (but questionable) savings in lieu of supplemental cash rebates.[b]
Managed care: Mandatory participation (South Carolina)	LAC recommended the state take steps to use Medicaid managed care to improve cost-efficiency and access to health care and explore mandatory participation in managed care.	*Cost Saving Strategies for the South Carolina Medicaid Program* (Oct. 2001)	Debate took place on recommendation to implement pilot programs for Medicaid managed care as a part of legislation to reorganize health and human services.
Health insurance options: Medicaid buy-in (Florida)	OPPAGA described how a Medicaid buy-in program could increase access to care and the feasibility of redesigning the state's Medically Needy program to a buy-in program.	*A Medicaid Buy-In Program Would Increase Health Care Access for the Uninsured But Also Increase State Costs* (Dec. 2005)	No legislative action.[b]

Health insurance options: Premium Payment Program (South Carolina)	LAC recommended expanding the Health Insurance Premium Payment program to avoid Medicaid costs.	*Cost Saving Strategies for the South Carolina Medicaid Program* (Oct. 2001)	No legislative action.[b]
Cost-saving initiatives: Impact of budget reductions (Florida)	OPPAGA reported whether the state achieved expected Medicaid savings from previously enacted law and budget changes.	*Expected Medicaid Savings Unrealized; Performance, Cost Information Not Timely for Legislative Purposes* (Nov. 2001)	Budget recommendations submitted by legislative staff.
		Medicaid Should Improve Cost Reduction Reporting and Monitoring of Health Processes and Outcomes (Aug. 2004)	Budget recommendations submitted by legislative staff.
Cost-saving initiatives: Recipient cost sharing (South Carolina)	LAC recommended expanding cost sharing with recipients to help limit Medicaid program costs.	*Options for Medicaid Cost Containment* (Jan. 2003)	No legislative action.[b]

[a]A small portion of the reported budget reduction was linked to other pharmacy controls.

[b]Reports that were not used by the legislature in the context described here were often used by state agencies to improve program operations.

[c]Pedigree papers are a written sales history that traces each drug back to its initial manufacturer. This provides an audit trail that contains specific sales transaction information, including the name and address of each previous purchaser of the drug.

Florida's Experience. OPPAGA's experience with its reviews of the Medicaid prescription drug program illustrates how strategies to increase the use of evaluators' work interact with other conditions to produce policy change. Florida statute directed OPPAGA to review the Medicaid program and report to the legislature during the 2001 session. At that time, Florida's Medicaid program served an average of 1.2 million clients monthly, and annual expenditures totaled $7.8 billion. The program was facing an estimated $640.6 million shortfall by the end of the year.

To identify the most critical issues facing the Medicaid program and ensure that the evaluation would be useful to the legislature, OPPAGA met with legislative policy and fiscal committee staff to identify specific areas of interest and concern. After meeting with Florida Medicaid agency staff and other stakeholders, OPPAGA met again with legislative staff to clarify the areas of focus for the review. From these discussions, OPPAGA identified four areas of concern to Florida's legislature, one of them the rising cost of Medicaid prescription drugs. The report on the Medicaid prescription drug program demonstrated the rapid increase in prescription drug costs as a major contributor to the projected deficit in the Medicaid budget.

Since 2001, OPPAGA has issued three reports on Medicaid prescription drugs and has made several policy recommendations that the legislature implemented. In making these recommendations, OPPAGA demonstrated how proposed changes would be expected to affect the costs of Medicaid prescription drugs. It also estimated savings that would occur if the legislature established a Medicaid preferred drug list (PDL) with mandatory manufacturer supplemental cash rebates; changed the state's pharmacy reimbursement formula; repealed the policy to allow drug manufacturers to provide services such as disease management in lieu of paying supplemental cash rebates; included drugs on the list that were initially exempt; and expanded the state's maximum pricing for generic drugs. These recommendations were feasible, could be implemented with little or no cost increase when compared to the potential cost savings, had clearly defined benefits, represented strategies that had been successfully used in other states or the private sector, and were not expected to limit recipient access to needed prescription drugs. These features helped increase legislators' confidence in the viability of the recommended policy changes.

The political environment at this time also favored change. Because of the significance of the continuing growth in Medicaid prescription drug costs, Florida's legislature was resolved to address this issue. Even so, the legislature was somewhat divided over how to fix the problem. There had been prior discussions related to whether to establish a PDL, but no action had been taken. OPPAGA's report provided the information needed for the legislature to make this decision. Thus, by informing the legislature and presenting recommendations that estimated cost savings, OPPAGA supported the existing political environment that was ready to address the issue.

To promote use of the Medicaid pharmacy reports, OPPAGA ensured that legislators and legislative staff received information needed for decision making in time for them to consider evaluation findings and recommendations. OPPAGA made the 2001 Medicaid prescription drug report available just before the legislative session. During that session, the office made several presentations before legislative policy and fiscal committees. Thus, legislators had sufficient time to consider the recommendations and opportunities to ask additional questions.

OPPAGA also discusses preliminary findings with legislative committee staff, ensuring that critical information is available to assist policymakers. An example pertains to the OPPAGA 2004 disease management report that described the failure of an existing PDL policy allowing drug manufacturers to provide services such as disease management (specialized services to individuals with chronic diseases to improve health outcomes and reduce health care costs) in lieu of paying the state supplemental cash rebates for brand-name prescription drugs. In this situation, certain drug manufacturers had guaranteed the state would save $64.2 million. OPPAGA analysis demonstrated that estimates of cost savings attributable to disease management were overstated, suggesting the legislature should again consider requiring all drug manufacturers to pay cash rebates to the state. OPPAGA briefed legislative staff on the results and implications of the analysis of drug manufacturers' cost-savings estimates prior to report publication. Sharing this information with legislative staff allowed them to draft an amendment to state law that would redact existing legislation and prepared them to file legislation on the day OPPAGA officially released the draft report.

Despite these examples of use, the Florida legislature has not acted on all of OPPAGA's Medicaid reports. In some instances, this was because recommendations directed the state Medicaid agency to address specific concerns that did not require legislative action in order for the agency to implement them. In other instances, the legislature did not act because of timing or conditions within the political environment. For example, the 2001 study on Medicaid's disease management initiative reported that expected cost savings had not been realized and that little evidence existed to demonstrate that individuals with chronic conditions experienced improved outcomes. Although the disease management issue was identified by legislators as important, the report received little attention. OPPAGA believes this was because the political environment at that time did not support making changes to Medicaid disease management, based on the expectation that the program would at some future point fulfill the promise of helping individuals manage their chronic conditions and result in better health outcomes.

South Carolina's Experience. In March 2000, 49 of South Carolina's 124 House members requested an audit of the Medicaid program due to "their concerns of tremendous program cost overruns and mismanagement." At that time, the state's Medicaid agency reported a potential deficit of $63.7 million, mostly due to the increase in the number of recipients and the loss of a funding source due to changes in federal law. The request of the General Assembly (South Carolina's legislature) focused on six issues, which LAC addressed in its 2001 and 2003 reports.

To ensure that LAC addressed the concerns of the legislature and to exchange information, LAC had discussions with legislative staff throughout the evaluation process. Through these discussions, LAC determined that the most important issues were program integrity and management of the prescription drug program. The 2001 report recommended several changes to both the program integrity division and the prescription drug program. In 2001, the General Assembly passed budget provisos requiring expansion of program integrity efforts and offsetting the increased costs with collections. However, the General Assembly did not address the recommendations concerning prescription drugs.

The South Carolina legislature needed information in January 2001, when it began to work on the state budget, but LAC did not publish the first Medicaid evaluation report until February 2001. However, LAC briefed members and staff of the House Ways and Means committee in January on the content of the report and provided a copy of the final report prior to its publication. As a result, the legislature proposed eight new budget provisos and reduced the Medicaid budget by $4.7 million. If LAC had not made information available prior to the budget cycle, the information would have been outdated and of little use to legislators by the next session.

Even when using strategies to promote legislative use of information provided in LAC reports, recommendations are not always implemented immediately after a report is released. Although the recommendations for changes to the prescription drug program were not addressed in the 2001 legislative session, LAC again reviewed the program in 2002 at the request of five senators. For this study, it reported on the experiences of other states, including Florida, in controlling costs in the state's prescription drug program. Based on the examples of other states, LAC estimated that South Carolina could save $12.8 million in state funds annually if it implemented a PDL. LAC released the report in January 2003, as requested by the senators, at the beginning of the state budget process. As a result of recommending policies that had been successfully used in other states and identifying the potential cost savings in time for legislators to use the information, LAC recommendations for prescription drugs were implemented by the General Assembly in the 2003 legislative session.

In the January 2003 Medicaid evaluation report, LAC also recommended changes to state law and state funding regarding long-term care to encourage more use of home and community-based care and less use of nursing homes.

At that time South Carolina had 3,600 people waiting for community-based care compared to only 281 waiting for nursing homes. Despite an average annual cost per recipient of $10,257 for community-based care and $21,452 for nursing home care, the General Assembly did not make any changes to state law or its funding of long-term care. The difficulty in balancing the nursing home providers' concerns over the loss of funding with the community long-term care providers' need for increased funding from a limited Medicaid budget prevented the General Assembly from acting on LAC's recommendations.

Conclusion

Evaluators can increase the likelihood that policymakers will use evaluation results by taking an active role in focusing research toward policymakers' concerns, developing reasonable and achievable policy recommendations, and ensuring timely dissemination of information for decision making.

With these conditions in mind, evaluators working in policy environments could periodically revisit the practices or strategies they use to ensure that reports meet policymakers' needs. They can track how policymakers use their reports and interview or survey policymakers and their staff to discuss ways to make reports more useful, keeping in mind issues related to problem definition, policy alternatives, and timing. Evaluators also should be mindful of the political environment. Although they have no control over this environment, evaluators can facilitate the use of their work by ensuring that policymakers have the information they need when the prevailing environment becomes more amenable to policy change.

References

Berry, F., Turcotte, J., and Latham, S. "Program Evaluation in State Legislatures: Professional Services Delivered in a Complex Competitive Environment." In R. Mohan, D. J. Bernstein, and M. D. Whitsett (eds.), *Responding to Sponsors and Stakeholders in Complex Evaluation Environments*. New Directions in Evaluation, no. 95. San Francisco: Jossey-Bass, 2002.

Bezruki, D., Mueller, J., and McKim, K. "Legislative Utilization of Evaluations." In R. K. Jonas (ed.), *Legislative Program Evaluation: Utilization-Driven Research for Decision Makers*. New Directions in Evaluation, no. 81. San Francisco: Jossey-Bass, 1999.

Grob, G. F. "Writing for Impact." In J. S. Wholey, H. P. Hatry, and K. E. Newcomer (eds.), *Handbook of Practical Program Evaluation*. (2nd ed.) San Francisco: Jossey-Bass, 2004.

Kingdon, J. W. *Agendas, Alternatives, and Public Policies*. (2nd ed.) New York: HarperCollins, 1995.

Mohan, R., Bernstein, D. J., and Whitsett, M. D. (eds.). *Responding to Sponsors and Stakeholders in Complex Evaluation Environments*. New Directions in Evaluation, no. 95. San Francisco: Jossey-Bass, 2002.

Palumbo, D. J. "Politics and Evaluation." In D. J. Palumbo (ed.), *The Politics of Evaluation.* Thousand Oaks, Calif.: Sage, 1987.
Patton, M. Q. *Utilization-Focused Evaluation: The New Century Text.* (3rd ed.) Thousand Oaks, Calif.: Sage, 1997.

YVONNE BIGOS is a chief analyst with the Florida legislature's Office of Program Policy Analysis and Government Accountability.

JENNIFER JOHNSON is a senior analyst with the Florida legislature's Office of Program Policy Analysis and Government Accountability.

RAE HENDLIN is a senior analyst with the Florida legislature's Office of Program Policy Analysis and Government Accountability.

STEVE HARKREADER is a chief analyst with the Florida legislature's Office of Program Policy Analysis and Government Accountability.

ANDREA TRUITT is general counsel for South Carolina's Legislative Audit Council.

5

This chapter describes the experience of an auditor's office in providing practical solutions to a long-term problem involving county jails.

A Utilization-Focused Approach to Evaluation by a Performance Audit Agency

Ron Perry, Bob Thomas, Elizabeth DuBois, Rob McGowan

For years, spending by the King County (Seattle, Washington) corrections department consumed a growing share of the county operating budget, and the department accrued a backlog of needed capital investments. At the same time, there was a history of mistrust between the county council and department management, which centered on whether the department's budget requests were fully justified and whether the department was operating as efficiently as possible. The department was frustrated that its efforts at efficiency were going unrecognized. It was also concerned that it had suffered budget cuts that could not be sustained and that essential capital projects continued to be unfunded.

The approach of the King County Auditor's Office was to level the playing field of knowledge by analyzing the reasons for budget growth and the need for capital projects. It did this by engaging key stakeholders and developing and using detailed cost models. These models helped to explain the in-depth operations of the county jails and the potential costs and benefits of implementing operational and capital improvements.

The success of the project, however, required far more than the technical work on modeling. In an environment in which a history of mutual mistrust existed between the corrections department and the county council, it was essential to include the key stakeholders in each stage of the analyses and to assure these stakeholders that the analyses were thorough

WILEY InterScience® DISCOVER SOMETHING GREAT

NEW DIRECTIONS FOR EVALUATION, no. 112, Winter 2006 © Wiley Periodicals, Inc.
Published online in Wiley InterScience (www.interscience.wiley.com) • DOI: 10.1002/ev.208

and objective. These stakeholders were the Department of Adult and Juvenile Detention, the county's Office of Management and Budget, and staff of the Metropolitan King County Council. Audit team members acted as honest brokers, researching questions in an open manner, facilitating dialogue, and inviting agency and budget staff to review the audit staff's work at every juncture. Although jail staff were closely involved in the study from the beginning, the audit staff's analyses were conducted independently and in accordance with government auditing standards. The role of the auditors included verifying the information provided to them about jail operations, developing cost models, and testing the models to ensure that they accurately portrayed operations and could be used for decision making.

An important lesson for the field of evaluation is that a performance audit agency can be involved in the development and implementation of management tools or models, while maintaining its necessary independence as required by generally accepted government auditing standards (U.S. Government Accountability Office, 2003). This is in contrast to the more common role of audit agencies, whereby they limit themselves to evaluating performance while avoiding involvement in implementation. This reluctance is not due to any actual impairments that result from engaging in this kind of evaluation but is rooted in the traditional approach to auditing. Thus, this project provides an important example of how a performance audit agency can ensure that its work is relevant and has immediate, practical application while maintaining its role in providing independent oversight.

Barriers to Utilization-Focused Evaluations by Performance Audit Agencies

In the third edition of his seminal work on utilization-focused evaluation, Michael Patton (1997) describes how the broader field of program evaluation, rooted in academic tradition, has struggled to overcome an aloofness that has prevented it from being more useful. He points out that the academic focus on technical quality and methodological rigor, while important or even essential, cannot be the sole emphasis of evaluation if evaluation is to be relevant to policymakers and other stakeholders. He reminded his readers that one of the seven deadly sins in evaluation is to wait until the findings are known before identifying intended users and potential uses. In contrast to the more traditional emphasis of program evaluation, Patton defines utilization-focused evaluation as "evaluation done for and with specific, intended primary users for specific, intended uses" (p. 23).

Within the narrower field of legislative program evaluation, another kind of aloofness can inhibit the production of work that is highly useful to stakeholders. Evident particularly among legislative audit agencies charged with conducting performance reviews, this kind of aloofness is expressed in terms of organizational independence. It has its origins in traditional auditing standards related to exercising objective and impartial judgment and the principle that auditors must never audit their own work (U.S. Government Accountability Office, 2003).

From a practical standpoint, the traditional focus on ensuring independence has led agencies conducting legislative audits to avoid utilization-focused strategies and overlook the benefits of engaging stakeholders. Ironically this has meant that they have especially avoided engaging the agency that is the subject of the audit itself. Too often, following these traditions has meant that auditors do not produce tools the audited agency can employ, based on a fear that a subsequent audit might involve a review of such tools, creating a real or perceived conflict of interest. This has limited the impact that performance audit analysis can have on improving government performance and accountability.

In Chapter Two of this volume, VanLandingham finds that audit agencies located within traditional auditing units (such as auditor generals) and those that have adopted Government Auditing Standards (including agencies that report to legislative committees) tend not to employ utilization strategies suggested in the professional literature. Due to organizational design and research norms, such agencies are not taking advantage of the strategies available to them. Our experience in working with auditors and auditing agencies around the country echoes VanLandingham's finding. We are also aware of what a typical response from a legislative audit or evaluation agency might be to that finding: they have no choice in the matter. They may point out that they are statutorily required to follow Government Auditing Standards, and, as the standards prescribe, they must be free in both fact and in appearance from any impairments to independence.

Overcoming the Barriers to Utilization

An alternative view offered in this chapter is that engaging stakeholders, especially the audited agency, is not only highly desirable but can be done without compromising independence. An additional observation is that some situations in auditing naturally and inevitably give rise to auditors' evaluating their own work, a fact that the Government Auditing Standards do not adequately address. This occurs, for example, when auditors conduct follow-up reviews or when they audit the same agency or program more than once. One of the first things that auditors do in such situations, as stipulated in the standards, is to review any work of significance from the previous audit. The standard reads: "Auditors should consider the results of previous audits and attestation engagements and follow up on known significant findings and recommendations that directly relate to the objectives of the audit being undertaken" (U.S. Government Accountability Office, 2003, 4.14).

In many instances, this will involve reviewing the analysis and evidence from the previous performance audit. When this is done, the possibility exists that mistakes, omissions, or other shortcomings from the previous work will be found, creating a potential conflict of interest. Another potential circumstance is that the audited agency will have used analytical tools developed during the previous audit, a situation that again puts the auditors conducting the follow-up work in the position of auditing their own work or that of their colleagues. Recognizing these inherent conflicts, the perspective offered in this chapter is that such issues should be confronted and dealt with directly rather than avoided or ignored. It is beneficial if mistakes or omissions can be found; otherwise they cannot be corrected. It is also desirable that analytical tools developed during the course of an evaluation or audit be used if they can add value.

We believe we are in good company in taking this position. The guidance of the Government Accountability Office (GAO) on this subject has been evolving. For example, the 2003 revision of the Government Auditing Standards expanded the definition of performance audits to include "prospective analyses" (2.13). This revision acknowledges that analytical modeling and forecasting can provide valuable information to decision makers about the potential costs and impacts of various alternatives. Similar to the retrospective focus the audit profession has traditionally placed on evaluating the past and current performance of public entities, it is equally important that auditors and evaluators hold these entities accountable for how accurately and effectively they make decisions about the future, or prospective, direction of public programs. The auditing standards also clearly state that the provision of tools and methodologies to the management of an audited agency should not be considered an impairment of an auditor's independence, provided that the agency's management policy choices and decision-making are not supplanted.

The following evaluation examples describe how utilization-driven evaluation is being conducted by a local government auditing agency. Although these evaluations may diverge somewhat from conventional audit approaches, we describe how they have nevertheless been conducted within the framework of Government Auditing Standards.

The Utilization-Focused Series of Jail Special Studies

The King County Auditor's Office analyzed jail operations and capital projects in a series of special studies that began in 2002 and are ongoing. The analytical core elements of the studies have been cost models developed by the auditor's office. From the beginning, we envisioned that the success of our efforts would be enhanced if our work embodied the following characteristics:

- *Be results driven.* A primary goal was to develop objective analytical tools to be used by the auditor's office, department management, the county budget office, and council staff in order to answer questions about existing operations, policies, and costs. Another aim was to identify a way to improve the quality and accuracy of available data to help the county council and department management make informed policy choices. The analysis we conducted throughout was oriented toward implementation (utilization) of these models and analyses and did not follow the traditional path of compliance or management control audits.

- *Be forward thinking.* Our cost models and related analyses were designed with the capability to simulate future alternative scenarios and perform sensitivity analyses. Our intent was to research and develop new, objective management tools and analyses that would help all stakeholders plan for the future. This is in contrast to the more typical audit approach of retrospectively evaluating program performance according to a set of established standards or performance criteria.
- *Be inclusive.* Including stakeholders in the development of the models and subsequent analyses played a key role in obtaining their acceptance of the objective management tools. Rather than keeping our distance from the agencies, common practice in traditional auditing, we chose to engage and include the stakeholders. This not only strengthened the accuracy, integrity, and relevance of our findings and recommendations, but also enhanced the sense of trust the stakeholders had in the auditor's office. Far from raising concerns about our objectivity, this inclusiveness and transparency added a measure of credibility that increased the project's impact and helped ensure our tools were used.

The Special Studies

The special studies had four phases.

Phase I: Cost Study. In 2002 the Metropolitan King County Council asked the King County auditor to examine the reasons for rising operational costs in the jails despite a drop in inmate populations. Between 1994 and 2000, both the inmate population and the costs of housing those inmates in King County jails grew steadily. However, as shown in Figure 5.1, in 2000 the inmate population began to drop, while the jails' costs continued to grow.

This upward trend came at a time when King County was facing a series of significant revenue shortfalls, in the range of $40 million to $50 million per year, or approximately 10 percent of the county's general fund. Also, because of the council's and budget staff's limited oversight and understanding of jail operations, previous fiscal decisions had been largely reactive to the demands of jail management and the need to house a growing inmate population. In addition, the county's criminal justice policy was undergoing a significant change, with a new emphasis on treatment and alternatives to incarceration.

In this context, the council asked the auditor's office for a detailed analysis of jail costs to improve its ability to strategically manage future changes in jail populations and costs and to better integrate jail operations

Figure 5.1. Secure-Detention Budget and Average Daily Population (ADP)

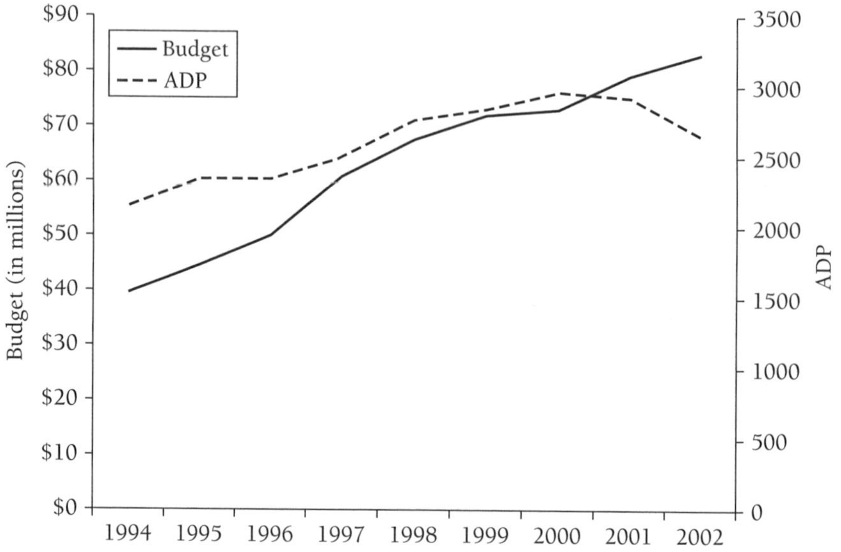

Source: King County Auditor's Office analysis and Department of Adult and Juvenile Detention population reports.

with the county's long-term criminal justice policy direction. In response, we developed a study work plan that addressed four key questions:

- What is driving jail costs?
- How are costs affected by changes in the inmate population?
- What is included in the costs of jail operations?
- What can be done to control costs?

To answer these questions, we began by studying jail operations, policies and procedures, staffing plans, and facility designs and then analyzed their underlying costs. We next developed a cost allocation model based on those operational policies and practices that included the total cost of operating a twenty-four-hour secure-detention facility. One of the most detailed components of the model focused on the security staffing for the residential housing units, the most staff- and cost-intensive area of jail operations. We designed the model to perform sensitivity analyses, or what-if scenarios, to see how costs would be affected by changes in inmate population, facility design, or staffing and operational policies. This was accomplished by identifying the points, or thresholds, at which these changes resulted in increases or decreases in staffing levels.

Developing the model required in-depth analysis of operations, policies, and costs that helped us arrive at a detailed understanding of the factors driving adult detention operating costs and to distinguish between fixed and varied costs with respect to changes in inmate population. For example, prior to the study, the Department of Adult and Juvenile Detention had cited constraints on its ability to reduce staffing costs and stated it was unable to improve staffing efficiency. We determined that some of these constraints were indeed substantial and beyond control. However, many were actually department practices that were not based on official department policy, operational standards, or adequate analysis, and others could be addressed through changes in policy. We integrated this information into the model so that managers and decision makers could see the operational and cost impacts of potential changes to these policies and practices.

This phase of our study determined that inmate population levels are the key cost driver, but other factors within the county's control also directly affect costs:

- Facility design constraints
- Changes in the costs of jail health services
- Efficiency of staffing practices
- Changes in the county's overhead costs

We approached the discussion of jail cost issues from a policy perspective, where decision makers could develop options for controlling costs and making strategic changes to jail operations. The department subsequently used the model to analyze alternative staffing options while preparing its 2004 budget submittal, and our analysis was also used extensively during several of the council's public budget review forums in 2004. In that same year, GAO invited our office to share our work as part of a panel on foresight analysis at the American Society for Public Administration's national conference in Portland, Oregon. GAO organized the panel to demonstrate how audit and evaluation organizations around the country are increasingly using prospective analysis and modeling in addition to more traditional, retrospective evaluation methods. This recognition of our efforts substantiated our position that utilization-focused evaluation methods can be effectively employed while working within the framework of government auditing standards.

Phase II: Jail Costs Follow-Up Study. Phase II focused on nonhousing aspects of jail operations. The objective of this phase was to determine if the costs of staffing or workload in areas other than residential housing were as sensitive to changes in inmate population as were housing costs. If so, we would update the model with thresholds for cost or staffing reductions for those areas.

Our work revealed that the nonhousing areas of the jails had varying levels of sensitivity to changes in inmate population. For example, work hours for court detail officers, who provide security escorts to inmates for court appearances, are closely related to variations in inmate population. (Our statistical analysis showed that almost 80 percent of the changes in court detail hours were explainable by changes in inmate population.) Hours for officers in intake, transfer, and release, who are responsible for booking inmates into jail and coordinating intake and release procedures, are only slightly related to inmate population levels.

As a result of our analysis, we recommended that the department develop a model that uses inmate population as a predictor of court detail transport hours. In the case of inmate transfer and release operations, we recommended that the department perform more analysis of the external factors affecting the number of bookings and releases and develop an appropriate workload-based staffing model.

Phase III: Integrated Security Project and Operational Master Plan Development. In 2002 the King County Executive developed a proposal for a $25-million integrated security project: replacement of the electronic security system in the county's aging, high-rise jail in downtown Seattle. Independent experts had concluded that the existing security systems, nearly obsolete and increasingly difficult to repair, were on the verge of catastrophic collapse. A challenge to the county and a major risk to the success of the project was the fact that the jail would have to continue in operation during the renovations.

Prior to submitting the security project budget to the county council for funding, the county executive engaged the services of a consultant to review the estimated $5.5 million in staffing costs associated with the project. These costs were based on the need to have additional correctional officers provide security for construction workers and to staff the housing units of temporarily displaced inmates.

The consultant's approach, similar to the work concurrently being done in the auditor's office, was to build a cost model. Whereas the original project budget model was static, in that it simply stated the costs of the staffing strategies proposed by the jail administrators, the consultant's model was an interactive simulation, allowing users to change assumptions about those strategies to see how the budget would change.

Creating a simulation required working closely with the jail staff and the security project planners, going over every operational and scheduling detail, and running and rerunning the model to ensure it accurately captured all major budget drivers. One of the immediate benefits of this approach was that in the process of conducting a sensitivity analysis, the consultant identified a major gap in the original budget, where $2.6 million in staffing costs had been inadvertently omitted. After correcting for this error, the true cost of the project was approximately $8.1 million instead of the originally assumed $5.5 million. This discovery presented a major setback to the project in terms of potential financial impact to the county. However, the modeling process also created the opportunity to identify new costs savings through different staffing strategies and operational changes.

When the auditor's office began its oversight of the security project, it worked with the consultant to update information and improve the model's ability to track and simulate proposed changes in the project. Ultimately use of the model helped to identify $5 million in savings, and the executive and legislative branches of county government employed the model as a tool for monitoring the progress of project implementation against the original assumptions. When the county council approved final funding for the security project, it adopted a recommendation from the auditor's office that called for independent testing of the security staffing practices during the project. An independent consultant subsequently verified the department's staffing plan.

In further developing and using this tool, the auditor's office followed Government Auditing Standards in ensuring that the information in the model was fact based and accurate, that the model faithfully simulated alternative staffing scenarios, and that the financial impacts were properly calculated. In no instance did the model itself, or the auditor's use of it, substitute for management decision making, thus ensuring we complied with Government Auditing Standard 3.13, which prohibits auditors from performing management functions. The model was not imposed but became a tool for identifying and quantifying the impacts of an array of potential operational decisions. Ultimately the county council and the executive had to make policy choices, taking into consideration the judgment of the corrections professionals.

The fact that agency and council staff were so closely involved in the development of the security project cost model and knew that its data and assumptions had been fully validated enhanced stakeholder confidence that the auditor's work was independent and objective. This recognition of the audit staff's growing expertise in jail operations contributed to the county council's decision to direct the auditor to assume a major role, beginning in 2003, in overseeing the development of the jail operational master plan, while continuing to review the budget and assumptions of the security project.

The auditor's office had a variety of roles in this next phase of work with the jail: oversight, quality assurance, and technical assistance. In selecting a consultant for the master plan, audit staff participated in developing the scope of work specified in the Request for Proposals and evaluating proposals submitted by bidders. During the course of preparing the master plan itself, auditors participated in an advisory work group that consisted of the consultants as well as staff from the executive agencies and the county council. This multiagency group reviewed technical issues and analyses, as well as drafts of individual chapters of the plan.

In addition, our review of the master plan report drafts corrected technical errors and critiqued the cost impact estimates of recommendations. Our analysis resulted in some significant modifications of cost figures and in one instance reversed the consultants' conclusions. The consultants acknowledged the expertise of the audit staff and their contribution to the quality and the content of the final master plan report. Our direct involvement in oversight of the master planning process resulted in a series of recommendations that, if implemented, could reduce jail operating costs by $3 million annually.

Phase IV: Monitoring Implementation. Following the completion and adoption of a master plan, and the final plans and budget for the security project, the county council gave the auditor a continuing oversight role in ensuring that security project implementation staffing costs were kept within budget and that long-term savings from the master plan's recommendations were on track to be implemented. Audit staff participated in multiagency advisory groups that oversee implementation of the two projects. This role is ongoing, as the time line for implementation extends well beyond 2008.

Conclusion

We believe that our multiphased study of jail costs and operations is an example of a highly effective utilization-focused evaluation conducted by an independent audit agency. It succeeded because it not only provided independently verified information and analysis of current jail operations and costs, but also developed objective tools that proved useful for prospective analysis by stakeholders. The innovative methods and approaches described in this chapter contributed to the overall success of the projects. The study yielded these positive outcomes because it was inclusive, results driven, and forward thinking.

Our experience on this project also leads us to conclude that working closely with agency management and developing tools and methodologies for their future use did not compromise the independence of the auditing function. Instead, our close involvement strengthened the integrity of the results and ultimate confidence in our work and helped ensure the results would be used. This level of trust was increased by the fact that we performed our work in compliance with Government Auditing Standards and that stakeholders comprehended the value of that effort.

If, in the future, we are in the position of reviewing our own work on the jails, we would acknowledge a potential impairment to our independence. However, we would manage it as we have done in all phases of the jail studies, as well as in every case where we conduct follow-up audits: acknowledge our past work and evaluate it objectively. We ensure that our additional analysis and review is open and transparent, involves stakeholders, and follows professional standards to help achieve accuracy and objectivity.

Furthermore, the prospective focus of the analytical components of the studies oriented the results toward implementation. Our objective was to improve the quality of the information held by county decision makers and strengthen their ability to plan for the future. The cost allocation models achieved this by providing an accurate cost context for the policy issues at hand. We are pleased to see that our approach is consistent with GAO's new emphasis on prospective analyses.

Finally, we conclude that by conducting implementation-focused work such as this, audit and evaluation offices have the potential to significantly strengthen the future planning and management capabilities of government. In the case of King County, our studies provided reliable information and new analytical tools that enhanced and strengthened the county's ability to manage the adult detention budget and refine its new criminal justice policy.

References

Patton, M. Q. *Utilization-Focused Evaluation: The New Century Text.* (3rd ed.) Thousand Oaks, Calif.: Sage, 1997.

U.S. Government Accountability Office. *Government Auditing Standards, 2003 Revision.* Washington, D.C.: U.S. General Accounting Office, 2003.

RON PERRY *is deputy county auditor in the King County Auditor's Office in Seattle.*

BOB THOMAS *is senior principal management auditor in the King County Auditor's Office in Seattle.*

ELIZABETH DUBOIS *is principal management auditor in the King County Auditor's Office in Seattle.*

ROB MCGOWAN *is principal management auditor in the King County Auditor's Office in Seattle.*

6

This chapter discusses the possible use of prospective evaluation by a legislative oversight agency. It illustrates reasons and methods for estimating future impacts of the No Child Left Behind Act.

Using a Crystal Ball Instead of a Rear-View Mirror: Helping State Legislators Assess the Future Impacts of Major Federal Legislation

Joel Alter, John Patterson

Typically, program evaluation agencies in the legislative branch of state government examine programs that have already been implemented. These evaluations often consider whether a program achieved the legislature's original goals or complied with statutory requirements. Program evaluations frequently determine whether executive branch agencies have made appropriate or cost-effective expenditures while operating a program.

For practical and political reasons, legislators may be reluctant to seek evaluations of young programs. Public officials may not want to initiate an evaluation until the implementing agency has had a fair chance to get a program up and running. In addition, legislators often recognize that it takes time for a program to establish a track record. If a program has been in place for only a few months, there may be a limited amount of data that evaluators can use to determine whether the program has met its goals. Legislators who advocated for creation of a program may fear a rush to judgment if an evaluation is undertaken too quickly. Although it is fairly uncommon for legislative program evaluation agencies to estimate programs' future impacts, this chapter suggests that such evaluations may be appropriate in certain circumstances.

WILEY InterScience® DISCOVER SOMETHING GREAT

NEW DIRECTIONS FOR EVALUATION, no. 112, Winter 2006 © Wiley Periodicals, Inc.
Published online in Wiley InterScience (www.interscience.wiley.com) • DOI: 10.1002/ev.209

Limited Past Use of Prospective Evaluation

Professional literature has often described program evaluation as an after-the-fact activity. For example, Poland (1974) said that program evaluation "involves a retrospective examination of program operations. It looks to the past to provide a guide to the future" (p. 333). A primer on evaluation in state and local government said that program evaluation "focuses on the past performance of ongoing or completed programs; thus it is primarily retrospective" (Hatry, Winnie, and Fisk, 1981, p. 4). Chelimsky (1985) observed that policy analysis focuses on "likely effects," while evaluation focuses on "actual effects" (pp. 6–7).

Nevertheless, program evaluation encompasses a wide variety of tools, approaches, and perspectives, including some that have a more forward-looking focus. The initial program evaluation standards developed by the Evaluation Research Society in the early 1980s identified front-end analysis, which focuses on a program's feasibility or resources prior to implementation, as one of six categories of evaluation. The society also said that formative evaluations, such as small-scale field tests, may be done in the early stages of new programs to help determine whether there is a need for modifications (Evaluation Research Society Standards Committee, 1982).

The U.S. Government Accountability Office (GAO) (1990) issued a guidebook on prospective evaluation methods. The guidebook described this type of evaluation as "a systematic method for providing the best possible information on, among other things, the likely outcomes of proposed programs, proposed legislation, the adequacy of proposed regulations, or top-priority problems" (p. 1). According to GAO, prospective evaluations often rely considerably on information about what has happened in the past, but it is appropriate for these evaluations to consider how programs might operate in the future under different conditions. GAO suggested that prospective evaluations be informed by empirical observations, logic, and practical considerations, which it referred to as "the triad of analysis" (p. 23).

Still, the use of prospective evaluation by policymakers has been somewhat limited at all levels of government. In its guidebook on prospective evaluation, GAO observed that "most proposed programs are put into operation—often nationwide—with little evaluative evidence attesting to their potential for success" (p. 90). Field tests, pilot projects, and policy analyses can take time to implement and analyze, and lawmakers may be unwilling to defer political action to await the results of such studies. In some cases, the impacts of legislation depend considerably on implementation decisions that follow enactment of the law, and it may be difficult to predict these choices beforehand.

Legislative staff can play important roles at various stages of the policy development and implementation process. Staff sometimes provide assistance to legislators in the early stages of policy development, outlining the advantages and disadvantages of alternative courses of action. Once legislators propose legislation, staff may be asked to estimate its fiscal implications. And once a legislative policy initiative has been fully implemented, there is certainly a role for legislative staff to conduct after-the-fact program evaluations. But there may also be times when it is appropriate for state lawmakers to seek prospective evaluations of programs that have been passed into law but are not yet implemented.

Minnesota's Evaluation of No Child Left Behind

The federal No Child Left Behind (NCLB) Act was enacted into law with bipartisan support in January 2002. It is the latest reauthorization of the federal Elementary and Secondary Education Act, an ongoing effort to improve public schools in the United States. NCLB is the nation's most significant educational reform in decades. The purpose of the act is to close the achievement gap between high- and low-performing students through improved accountability, expanded educational choices, and more funding.

Under NCLB, all students in public schools are supposed to be proficient in reading and math by 2014. To measure progress toward this goal, NCLB requires states to administer annual reading and math assessments in grades 3 through 8 and at one high school grade level. It also requires states to establish gradually increasing targets for schools, leading to 100 percent of students being proficient by 2014. States must report the extent to which their schools are achieving annual targets and making adequate yearly progress toward the goal of 100 percent proficiency.

In addition, NCLB holds individual schools accountable for the performance of the full student body plus eight specific subgroups: white, black, Asian, American Indian, Hispanic, limited-English, special education, and low-income students. In each school, each of these groups must meet the state's proficiency targets in both reading and math. Also, at least 95 percent of students in each group must take each test. Overall, each school must annually meet up to thirty-seven performance targets to achieve adequate yearly progress.

NCLB specifies sanctions for schools that fail to make adequate yearly progress. At schools that have underperformed for at least two consecutive years, school districts must offer parents the option of transferring their children to other schools. Following a third year of underperformance by a school, districts must also offer parents the option of enrolling their children in supplemental educational services, such as after-school tutoring. If schools continue to underperform in subsequent years, NCLB subjects them to corrective actions (such as replacement of staff or curriculum) or restructuring.

Legislative Request for the Study. In 2002, Minnesota elected a governor who was a strong supporter of the federal NCLB law. But during the 2003 legislative session, legislators from both major political parties expressed concern about the possible impact that NCLB might have on

Minnesota's education system. Although NCLB increased Minnesota's educational funding from the federal government by tens of millions of dollars, the act had the potential to impose significant new education costs.

Some legislators requested an independent review of NCLB by the Minnesota Office of the Legislative Auditor (OLA), a nonpartisan office that conducts evaluations on behalf of the legislature. A bipartisan legislative audit commission selects OLA's program evaluation topics. OLA staff informed the commission that it would be challenging to evaluate NCLB before it was fully implemented. Similarly, the chair of a legislative education committee questioned whether it would be feasible for the auditor's office to provide answers at this early stage to the questions posed in the office's research proposal. But most legislators consulted by OLA said that a study of NCLB's likely impact was too important to defer. Thus, a little more than a year after NCLB was signed into law, the legislative audit commission directed OLA to assess the act's likely impacts on Minnesota.

Methods. OLA's evaluation used three main research methods. First, it relied on a simulation to estimate for 2004 through 2014 how many schools would achieve adequate yearly progress under various scenarios. Second, OLA estimated future costs based on the results of the simulation, as well as information solicited from selected school districts and the state department of education. Third, OLA conducted a statewide survey of school superintendents (Minnesota Office of the Legislative Auditor, 2004).

OLA simulated the ability of schools to comply with NCLB based on (1) the NCLB requirements that existed in 2003, (2) Minnesota's statewide student test data from 2003, and (3) assumptions about future student achievement levels that ranged from "no improvement" to "high improvement" from the 2003 levels. The simulation focused on student achievement scores and did not consider other NCLB criteria that might cause a school to fail to make adequate yearly progress. Specifically, the simulation did not consider whether schools would comply with NCLB's requirements for attendance rates, graduation rates, or the percentage of students taking each test.

OLA limited the simulation to elementary schools for two reasons. First, the simulation used actual statewide test scores to help estimate future compliance with NCLB, and Minnesota had administered statewide student assessments in only grades 3 and 5 at the time of the analysis. Second, most schools in Minnesota that receive NCLB funding are elementary schools, and only schools that receive NCLB funding face sanctions for not achieving adequate yearly progress.

OLA contracted with the University of Minnesota's Office of Educational Accountability to conduct a simulation based on the model and assumptions specified by OLA. This research center within the university was a regular user of Minnesota's student test data and was well regarded by lawmakers and executive branch officials. The Office of Educational Accountability operates independent of the Minnesota Department of Education, the state agency with responsibility for administering NCLB.

The simulation used an approach known as sampling with replacement. For future school years, the simulation generated from each school's 2003 achievement data a new sample of tested students. Within a school, this approach resulted in random year-to-year fluctuations in the number of students tested, the number of students in each subgroup, and the proficiency rate. Using this method, the simulation generated test scores for students in grades 3 through 6 and proficiency rates for each of the subgroups in each school. The simulation produced estimates of schools' compliance with NCLB requirements for school years 2004 through 2014.

In the second part of its prospective analysis, OLA estimated the cost of implementing the new requirements in the NCLB act. For these estimates, the simulation results helped determine the extent to which schools might be required by NCLB to implement school choice and supplemental educational services. In addition, OLA estimated other NCLB-related costs based largely on cost estimates obtained from the Minnesota Department of Education and nine school districts. To facilitate consistent data collection, OLA gave instructions to the department and districts regarding how to estimate these costs. Specifically, OLA identified over two hundred activities needed to carry out the NCLB act. NCLB's primary costs include (1) conducting additional testing, (2) offering students who attend failing schools the options of switching schools or receiving supplemental educational services, (3) requiring corrective action for schools that fail to make adequate yearly progress for four consecutive years and restructuring for schools that underperform for five years, and (4) improving the qualifications of teachers and aides.

Finally, to gauge local perspectives about NCLB's impact, OLA surveyed Minnesota's 342 school district superintendents. About 95 percent responded. School districts are at the front lines of NCLB implementation, and it seemed reasonable to determine the opinions of district leaders about the federal law's provisions and likelihood of success.

Findings. OLA's simulation model used three different scenarios regarding future student performance. OLA staff could not predict specific student achievement levels under NCLB, so they examined a wide range of possible outcomes. Under a "no improvement" scenario, OLA assumed no improvement in overall student achievement over the eleven-year period of NCLB's implementation. In other words, students and schools would perform, on average, at the same level at which they were performing in 2003. At the other extreme, OLA considered a "high-improvement" scenario based on the relatively large average annual improvements in proficiency that occurred in Minnesota over the 2000–03 period (an average annual increase in the proficiency rate of 2.54 percentage points). This scenario assumed that schools would continue to improve at this rate through 2014.

Staff from the Office of Educational Accountability expressed skepticism about the high-improvement assumption, noting that an unusually large increase in a single year (from 2002 to 2003) caused the relatively large three-year average increase and that previous research has suggested that it would be unusual to sustain large improvements in achievement over a long period of time. Because of skepticism about the 2002–03 increase, OLA added a third scenario that assumed a more modest increase in achievement consistent with Minnesota's statewide experience from 2000 to 2002 (an average annual increase in the proficiency rate of 0.57 percentage points). In fact, after OLA's report was released, the Minnesota Department of Education revealed that the 2002–03 increase was not as large as it had reported earlier due to an error in determining the proficiency rate.

Under the three scenarios, the simulations showed that between 80 and 100 percent of Minnesota's elementary schools would fail to make adequate yearly progress by 2014 (Figure 6.1). Clearly, helping every student become proficient would be a daunting task. For example, the high-improvement scenario in Figure 6.1 shows that a large proportion of schools could meet the NCLB proficiency standard by 2013 if they had large, steady gains in average student achievement. Still, most of these schools with steadily-growing achievement levels would be unable to comply with NCLB's ultimate goal of universal proficiency by 2014.

The analysis indicated that individual schools would typically fail to achieve adequate yearly progress because of the performance of numerous subgroups, not just one or two. By the 2014–15 school year, between 35 and 76 percent of schools receiving NCLB funding would face NCLB's most serious sanction, restructuring, and most other schools would face other types of NCLB sanctions.

Figure 6.1. Percentage of Elementary Schools Failing to Make Adequate Yearly Progress in Proficiency

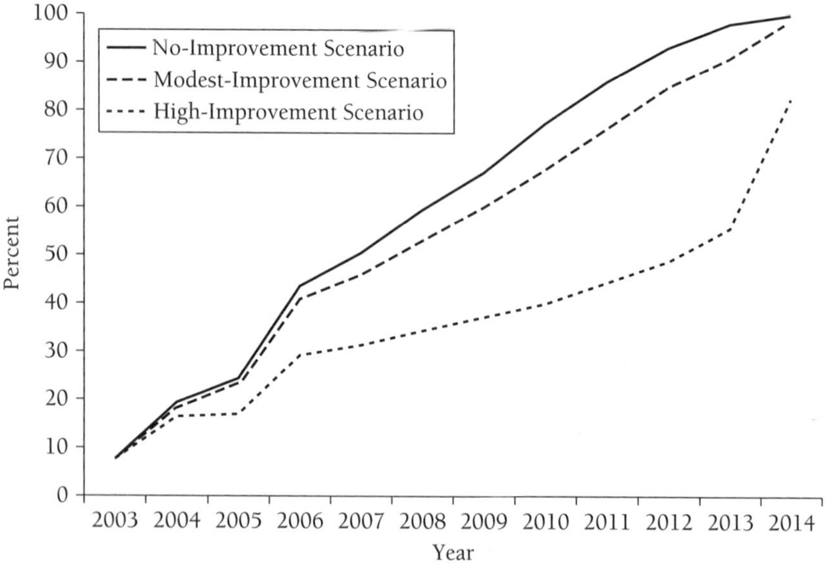

OLA found that the school failure rate rose over time under each scenario primarily because the proficiency targets set by Minnesota will increase each year. Specifically, the state's proficiency target rises from about 66 percent of students in 2003 to 100 percent in 2014. The assumptions about how students would actually perform on their tests did not greatly affect the overall conclusion that it would be difficult for schools to comply with NCLB's ambitious objectives.

Estimating NCLB's costs was particularly challenging because, at the time of OLA's analysis, Minnesota had not implemented many of NCLB's new requirements. In fact, Minnesota had not even decided how it was going to meet some of the new requirements. Thus, OLA estimated only the costs for which it had a reasonably solid basis for making future estimates: the testing, school choice, and supplemental services requirements.

OLA estimated that Minnesota's state and local costs for administering NCLB's newly required tests would total approximately $19 million annually. Although Minnesota had implemented (or planned to implement) several statewide tests before NCLB passed, the costs of some other tests were solely attributable to NCLB because they would not have been conducted without NCLB. For example, prior to NCLB, Minnesota planned to test students on a statewide basis in reading and math in grades 3, 5, 7, 10, and 11. NCLB then required statewide testing in grades 3 through 8 and at one high school grade level. Thus, the reading and math tests in grades 4, 6, and 8 were newly required under NCLB.

In addition, OLA estimated that Minnesota's school districts would spend up to $20 million annually to comply with NCLB's requirements for school choice and supplemental educational services. This estimate depended partly on the number of schools failing to make adequate yearly progress for at least two consecutive years. Under three scenarios with very different assumptions about student performance, OLA estimated that a large share of Minnesota's schools that receive NCLB funding would likely be required to provide school choice and supplemental educational services by 2014. OLA did not estimate the cost of more serious sanctions, such as corrective action and restructuring at schools that fail to make adequate yearly progress for four or five consecutive years, respectively—mainly because it was unclear what specific strategies would be pursued in schools subject to these sanctions.

Overall, OLA found that the cost of implementing the testing, school choice, and supplemental service requirements alone could reach nearly $40 million annually in Minnesota. In addition, OLA estimated that there would be potentially large (but hard-to-quantify) costs associated with the other NCLB requirements: those related to corrective action, school restructuring, and teacher and aide qualifications. Because of this, OLA concluded that it was quite plausible that new NCLB-related costs would exceed the $42 million increase in annual revenues that Minnesota was expected to receive under NCLB.

OLA's statewide survey of school district superintendents found general support for NCLB's emphasis on improving the achievement levels of all children, but most superintendents viewed the act as unrealistic, costly, and punitive. Only 17 percent of superintendents said that it was "likely" or "very likely" that their districts could help all students become proficient by 2014. These survey results were consistent with the OLA simulations that indicated that a high percentage of elementary schools would fail in making all students proficient by 2014.

The survey also revealed that superintendents had fundamental disagreements with some of NCLB's accountability requirements. For example, nearly three-fourths of superintendents said that special education and limited-English students, two of the subgroups for which schools are held accountable, should not be held to the same standards of academic proficiency as other students. For each of the various NCLB subgroups, a majority of superintendents said that schools should not be required to face the NCLB-prescribed consequences for the subgroup's persistent failure to make adequate yearly progress.

Superintendents also expressed considerable skepticism about NCLB's future impacts on their districts. Only 7 percent said that the educational benefits of NCLB would outweigh any adverse impacts the act would have on their districts. In addition, less than 3 percent of superintendents said that they expected their school district's share of the increased federal revenues to cover the cost of new spending required by NCLB.

Lessons

In its 1990 guidebook on prospective evaluation, GAO said that evaluators may wish to use this method to help develop appropriate recommendations for policymakers. Specifically, GAO suggested using a prospective evaluation approach in cases involving complex intergovernmental relationships, significant costs, major structure or management changes, or high stakes. In our view, these factors also led to legislative support for OLA's review of No Child Left Behind and could justify other prospective evaluations by state-level program evaluation agencies.

For example, the NCLB law has important implications for state and local agencies that were not comprehensively analyzed prior to the law's passage. Subsequent to the law's enactment, it was reasonable for state legislators to seek information to help them respond appropriately to this federal legislation. After the OLA report was issued, Minnesota lawmakers passed legislation that required the Minnesota Department of Education to seek waivers from various provisions of the federal NCLB act. The legislation required that if these waivers were not obtained by early 2007, the department would have to recommend whether the state should opt out of NCLB and forgo NCLB-related federal funding.

In addition, a before-the-fact evaluation of NCLB was justified by the program's potential impact on future education costs. Education is the largest area of expenditure by state governments, and Minnesota legislators worried that implementing NCLB's requirements could impose new fiscal burdens on state government and local school districts. Ultimately OLA determined that only certain NCLB-related costs could be estimated with confidence for future years, and it had no way of knowing whether there might be changes in the NCLB-related revenues that Minnesota would receive in the future. But based on cautious assumptions, the study showed why it was plausible that new costs imposed by NCLB could exceed Minnesota's new NCLB revenues.

Finally, NCLB had potentially significant consequences for Minnesota's education system, and this justified an evaluation early in the program's implementation process. Under NCLB, every public school faced new requirements that could affect day-to-day school operations, such as who would be authorized to teach and how student progress would be measured. Schools that did not meet NCLB's ambitious standards faced penalties that could lead to increased spending or changes in school staffing, curriculum, or management. In addition, school officials feared the impact on public opinion of having their schools labeled as underperforming. As the OLA evaluation concluded, there was good reason for educators to be concerned that many of Minnesota's schools would be unable to meet NCLB's increasingly strict requirements by 2014.

When the OLA report was released, the commissioner of Minnesota's state department of education criticized the report as "a doom-and-gloom statement that is more propaganda than objective reality" (Yecke, 2004, p. 6AA). Curiously, however, her main concern was not that the Office of the Legislative Auditor conducted a prospective evaluation to estimate the law's future impacts. Rather, she criticized the use of a methodology "based on the assumption that the law won't be changed for 11 years. . . . To assume that there will be no changes to this law over the course of 11 years is to ignore reality" (Yecke, 2004, p. 6AA).

However, OLA staff believed that it would have been highly speculative to try to predict future congressional actions. In response to the state education commissioner's criticism of the report, Minnesota's legislative auditor wrote to a legislative committee, "It is hard to see how we could have factored in future changes to the law. We would need to know what specific changes will be passed by the Congress and signed by the President and, unfortunately, we do not have that level of knowledge. Therefore, we think it is appropriate for us to base our analysis on the current requirements of No Child Left Behind" (Nobles, 2004).

It is likely that state legislatures will continue to use their in-house program evaluation agencies mainly to examine the actual outcomes of fully implemented programs and policies. Generally researchers can more reliably document what has already happened than estimate what might happen in the future. But when the stakes of programs are high, it may be appropriate for legislators to seek an early, independent assessment of likely outcomes. Legislative program evaluation agencies should be flexible enough to consider innovative—and occasionally nontraditional—ways of accommodating legislators' needs for information. Estimates of future impacts—if informed by past performance and guided by a reasonable range of assumptions about future performance—can be a powerful analytical tool to help state lawmakers.

References

Chelimsky, E. "Old Patterns and New Directions in Program Evaluation." In E. Chelimsky (ed.), *Program Evaluation: Patterns and Directions.* Washington, D.C.: American Society for Public Administration, 1985.

Evaluation Research Society Standards Committee. "Evaluation Research Society Standards for Program Evaluation." In P. H. Rossi (ed.), *Standards for Evaluation Practice.* New Directions for Program Evaluation, no. 15. San Francisco: Jossey-Bass, 1982.

Hatry, H. P., Winnie, R. E., and Fisk, D. M. *Practical Program Evaluation for State and Local Governments.* Washington, D.C.: Urban Institute Press, 1981.

Minnesota Office of the Legislative Auditor. *No Child Left Behind.* St. Paul: Minnesota Office of the Legislative Auditor, 2004.

Nobles, J. "Evaluation of No Child Left Behind." Memorandum to members of the Minnesota House of Representatives Committee on Education Policy, Mar. 1, 2004.

Poland, O. F. "Program Evaluation and Administrative Theory." *Public Administration Review,* 1974, *34*(4), 333–338.

U.S. Government Accountability Office. *Prospective Evaluation Methods: The Prospective Evaluation Synthesis.* Washington, D.C.: Government Printing Office, 1990.

Yecke, C. P. "Educators Call Chicken Little to Mind." *Star Tribune (Minneapolis-St. Paul),* Aug. 29, 2004, p. 6AA.

JOEL ALTER and JOHN PATTERSON manage program evaluations for the Minnesota Office of the Legislative Auditor.

7

Performance measurement can benefit evaluation by clarifying policy intent, program goals, and performance expectations and by facilitating systematic data collection. Because policymakers tend to support performance measurement for accountability purposes, linking performance measurement to evaluation has the potential of increasing evaluation use among policymakers.

Increasing Evaluation Use Among Policymakers Through Performance Measurement

Rakesh Mohan, Minakshi Tikoo, Stanley Capela, David J. Bernstein

In times of budget shortfalls and ever increasing demand for transparency and accountability for use of tax dollars in the public sector, it is clear that the use and influence of performance measurement has increased (Governmental Accounting Standards Board, 2003; Mayne, 2004; Mohan, 2006; National Conference of State Legislatures, 2003; Newcomer, Jennings, Broom, and Lomax, 2002). *Performance measurement* is a "fairly inclusive term that may refer to the routine measurement of program inputs, outputs, intermediate outcomes, or end outcomes" (Newcomer 1997, p. 7). In addition to the federal government, all states and most local governments in the United States use some form of performance measurement (U.S. Government Accountability Office, 2002; Melkers and Willoughby, 2004, 2005).

In spite of its popularity, performance measurement by itself has limited utility; it can be used primarily for monitoring programs in terms of their resources, outputs, and results. What performance measurement cannot do is serve as a substitute or a shortcut for evaluation, which involves making a value judgment about the worth of a policy or program. Identifying and

---

The views expressed in this article are the authors' and do not necessarily represent those of the Office of Performance Evaluations or the Idaho legislature.

WILEY InterScience® DISCOVER SOMETHING GREAT

NEW DIRECTIONS FOR EVALUATION, no. 112, Winter 2006 © Wiley Periodicals, Inc.
Published online in Wiley InterScience (www.interscience.wiley.com) • DOI: 10.1002/ev.210

communicating why a program works or does not work falls in the realm of evaluation (Wholey and Newcomer, 1997). During the past decade, much discussion has taken place relating to the benefits and limitations of performance measurement. Perrin (1998) initiated one such debate, triggering responses from Bernstein (1999) and Winston (1999), followed by a rebuttal from Perrin (1999).

The Government Performance and Results Act of 1993 recognizes the relationship between performance measurement and evaluation by requiring federal agencies in the United States to identify and conduct program evaluations to help understand changes being observed in program performance as monitored by performance measurement activities. Specifically, performance measurement can offer assistance to evaluators by clarifying policy intent, program goals, and performance expectations and by facilitating systematic data collection. These activities are interrelated and are necessary components to any evaluation. Because policymakers tend to support performance measurement for accountability purposes—as evidenced by the fact that governments at all three levels in the United States have passed legislation over the past decade requiring some form of performance measurement in government—linking performance measurement to evaluation has the potential of increasing evaluation use among policymakers.

Need for Shared Understanding of Purpose and Systematic Data Collection

The extent to which public policies are articulated through statutes, rules, and other formal mechanisms is a predictor of successful policy implementation (Mazmanian and Sabatier, 1981). Lack of clear articulation leads to multiple interpretations of policy intent, program goals, and performance expectations among policymakers, program officials, and other stakeholders. This multiplicity of interpretation not only hinders the implementation of the policy, but also presents challenges to evaluators on how to assess the impact of that policy when there are no commonly agreed on or generally accepted criteria against which to measure program results.

An evaluation always needs data to assess how a program is doing with respect to its purpose and goals. Lack of clarity about the purpose and goals contributes to an inability to track needed data or to tracking data that are not useful in assessing impact. Of course, evaluators can construct new data using file reviews, site visits, surveys, focus groups, and interviews, but such data collection takes additional resources in terms of money and time. In dynamic public policy environments, policymakers often do not have the luxury to wait for information they need today. It is better for both a program's implementation and its evaluation if data aligned with commonly understood purposes and goals are collected in an ongoing and systematic way through performance measurement.

Three examples illustrate how the lack of clarity of policy intent, program goals, and performance expectations contributed to the poor implementation of programs and the inability of evaluators to assess the impact of those programs.

Jobs for the Environment. This Washington State program was established in the early 1990s to produce measurable improvements in water quality and provide economic stability in the targeted areas through environmental and forest restoration projects conducted by displaced natural resource workers. A legislative study found that the impact of the program could not be measured because legislative intent for the program was not clear and criteria against which the program would be held accountable were not identified. Furthermore, program staff did not collect necessary data, including long-term monitoring of its environmental restoration projects, for use in assessing impact (Washington Legislature, 1998).

Data collected by program staff included types and amount of work performed, types of jobs created, amount of wages paid, and number of people employed. In addition, program staff relied on some anecdotal information about the program's usefulness to the environment and the displaced natural resource workers. Although this information was helpful in tracking program activities and expenditures, it did not enable evaluators to assess whether the program produced measurable improvements in water quality and provided economic stability in the targeted areas.

Linked Deposit. A legislative review of Washington's Linked Deposit program, which provided reduced-interest loans to minority- and women-owned small businesses through participating banks, found that the program's impact could not be measured for two reasons. First, statutes, rules, and other formal policy documents did not specify what was expected of the program in terms of performance. Second, data necessary to measure the program's impact were not tracked (Washington Legislature, 1999).

As outlined in statutes, the purpose of the program was to increase access to business capital for the state's minority- and women-owned businesses. However, access to capital was not defined, nor were any criteria specified regarding which minority- or women-owned businesses would qualify for the program. Program staff basically tracked two pieces of information, loan recipient and amount, plus some anecdotal information from loan recipients claiming the program was of benefit to them. These data sets were not sufficient to assess the program's impact in improving access to business capital for minority- and women-owned businesses.

Educational Technology Initiative. A legislative study found that the statewide plan for implementing the Idaho Educational Technology Initiative of 1994 had not specified the criteria for judging progress. The purpose of the initiative was to promote the effective use of learning technologies in public schools. Program staff measured progress by tracking amounts of money given in grants to school districts for technology, as well as numbers of computers and related equipment purchased. Like the programs in the previous two examples, the educational technology initiative lacked explicit performance expectations and criteria for measuring whether those expectations were met. The study recommended that the program focus on improving cost-effectiveness of its technology investments and readiness of individual school districts to provide and integrate technology in schools (Idaho Legislature, 2005).

Using Performance Measurement to Build a Foundation for Evaluation

The first step in implementing a comprehensive performance measurement system is to develop a strategic plan for the program that clarifies policy intent, establishes and prioritizes program goals, and lays out performance expectations. To be effective, this process should involve program officials, policymakers, and other key stakeholders. Collectively, they need to reach a reasonable level of agreement on policy intent, program goals, and performance expectations (Poister, 2004; Wholey, 1999).

Subsequent steps of a performance measurement system include developing performance indicators that reflect policy intent, program goals, and performance expectations; developing a process for monitoring the program and systematically collecting data on the selected indicators; establishing a quality assurance process for data integrity; and designing a method for disseminating performance information to program officials, policymakers, and other key stakeholders (Poister, 2004; Wholey, 1999). Successful completion of these steps will lay the foundation for future evaluation of the program. Evaluators will be clear about policy intent, program goals, and performance expectations, and at least some data will be available to them for evaluating the program's impact.

Evaluators can play an important role in designing a performance measurement system by assisting program officials and policymakers. For example, evaluators can use logic models to help build common understanding about policy intent, program goals, and performance expectations, as well as identify linkages among inputs, outputs, and outcomes (McLaughlin and Jordan, 2004). Evaluators can also help with ensuring data integrity by encouraging agencies to integrate quality assurance steps as components of data collection processes. In essence, there is a symbiotic relationship between performance measurement and evaluation: evaluation methods can be used to help design a sound performance measurement system, which provides evaluators with performance criteria and data for assessing the program's impact.

Increasing Evaluation Use Among Policymakers

The symbiotic relationship between evaluation and performance measurement has potential for increasing evaluation use among policymakers. Evaluation is often perceived as a costly venture or a time-consuming academic exercise that has little value in the real world of policymaking and government operations (Sanders, 2003; Mayne, 2006; Wholey and Newcomer, 1997). In contrast, performance measurement often is used in government settings, and policymakers tend to support performance measurement for accountability purposes. Because there is a mutually beneficial relationship between evaluation and performance measurement, evaluators are presented with an opportunity to educate government program managers and policymakers about this relationship as part of a comprehensive accountability system (Bernstein, 1999).

As Mohan and Sullivan discussed in Chapter One, one way to communicate with policymakers is to be responsive to their information needs. Evaluators can elicit their input by involving them in reviewing performance information and providing feedback to program officials. Policymakers' feedback can shed light on policy intent, program goals, and performance expectations. Once policymakers are involved, it would be relatively easy to convince them that the use of performance information could help them make informed policy decisions. The use of performance information is likely to raise more questions about why a program works or does not work. The answers to such questions can then be found through evaluation.

An example from Idaho illustrates how policymakers could be involved in a performance measurement process. In 1993, the Idaho legislature had enacted legislation requiring strategic plans and annual performance reports from state agencies. The intent of this legislation was to improve agency performance and government accountability by providing performance information to the governor and the legislature as part of the executive budget. However, the process did not work for the legislature or the executive branch. Neither group of policymakers found the forthcoming information useful for making policy decisions or managing state programs. Furthermore, nonpartisan legislative staff had limited confidence in the accuracy, adequacy, and relevance of the information reported.

Based on the premise that easy access to accurate and meaningful performance information is fundamental to improving accountability in government, a 2004 legislative study recommended revising the existing process for collecting and reporting performance information (Idaho Legislature, 2004). Acting on this recommendation, the legislature unanimously passed a bill during the 2005 legislative session revising the state's performance measurement process. The governor subsequently signed the bill into law effective July 2005. Figure 7.1 illustrates the built-in legislative feedback

Figure 7.1. State-Level Performance Measurement Process with Policymaker Involvement

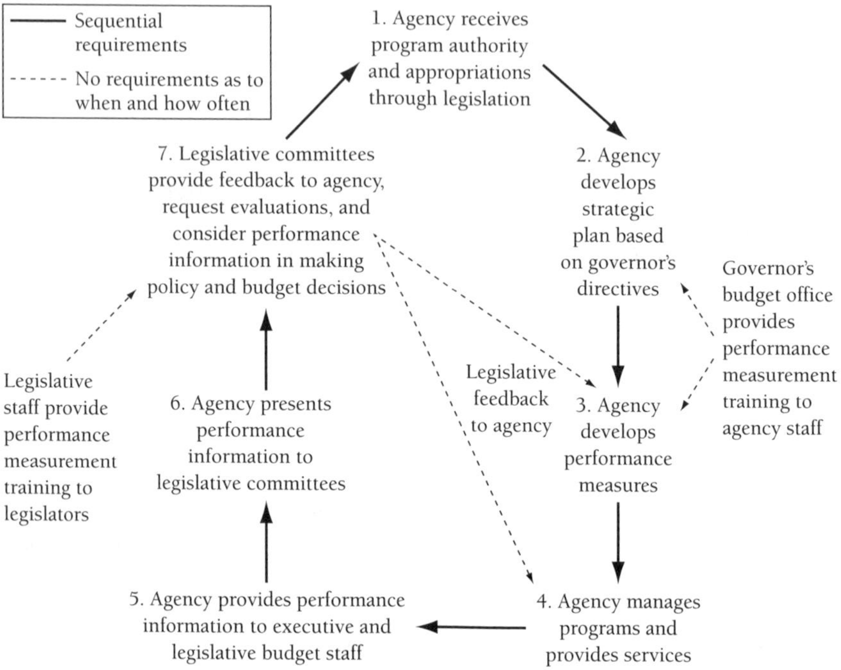

Source: Based on information presented in *Strategic Planning and Performance Measurement* (Idaho Legislature, 2004).

mechanism of the revised process, which includes the following key elements:

- Requires agencies to submit to the governor, as part of their strategic plan, an agency profile consisting of an overview and descriptions of core statutory functions, cases managed or key services provided, and performance highlights
- Requires that training be provided to legislators and state agency personnel on how to collect and report performance information
- Requires agencies to submit to the governor accurate and meaningful performance information containing key performance indicators with benchmarks and explanations
- Requires legislative policy committees to review agency performance information and provide feedback on the usefulness of performance information and what is expected of program officials in terms of accountability

The built-in legislative feedback mechanism is probably the strongest element of Idaho's process. It provides policymakers and program officials an ongoing opportunity to engage in a dialogue with each other on clarifying policy intent, program goals, and performance expectations. Through this process, they can reach a reasonable level of agreement on program priorities, goals, and expectations and regularly monitor program performance. Policymakers can also let program officials know whether the performance information is useful for accountability and policymaking purposes.

Conclusion

More and more governments are using performance measurement for improving accountability. Because stakes are high when performance measurement is used for making or judging public policies, evaluators should nurture a dialogue with government program managers and policymakers who are driving the use of performance measurement. This dialogue should focus on explaining the difference between performance measurement and evaluation and how both can be used in tandem to improve accountability and program effectiveness. Performance measurement builds the foundation for conducting future evaluation by clarifying policy intent, program goals, and performance expectations, as well as by facilitating systematic data collection. Evaluation then can be used to answer questions regarding why the program works or does not work and to assess its impact. By explaining this relationship between performance measurement and evaluation, evaluators can potentially increase the use of evaluation among policymakers.

A two-year executive session on public sector performance management at Harvard's Kennedy School of Government concluded in 2001 with a memorandum to government executives stating that performance goals and measurement are among the most powerful tools they have for advancing program priorities. They "can drive improved performance by clearly articulating performance goals and publicly reporting progress toward them. They can strengthen democracy, as well, because public goals and progress reports implicitly invite the public—and its elected representatives—to consider the appropriateness of the goals an agency selects" (Harvard University, 2001, p. 11).

References

Bernstein, D. J. "Comments on Perrin's Effective Use and Misuse of Performance Measurement." *American Journal of Evaluation*, 1999, *20*, 85–93.

Governmental Accounting Standards Board. *Reporting Performance Information: Suggested Criteria for Effective Communication*. Norwalk, Conn.: Governmental Accounting Standards Board, 2003.

Harvard University, John F. Kennedy School of Government. "A Memorandum to Government Executives from the Executive Session on Public Sector Performance

Management Regarding *Get Results Through Performance Management*." Cambridge, Mass.: Harvard University, 2001.

Idaho Legislature. *Strategic Planning and Performance Measurement*. Boise, Idaho: Office of Performance Evaluations, Dec. 2004.

Idaho Legislature. *Public Education Technology Initiatives*. Boise, Idaho: Office of Performance Evaluations, Jan. 2005.

Mayne, J. "Reporting on Outcomes: Setting Performance Expectations and Telling Performance Stories." *Canadian Journal of Program Evaluation*, 2004, *19*, 31–60.

Mayne, J. "Audit and Evaluation in Public Management: Challenges, Reforms, and Different Roles." *Canadian Journal of Program Evaluation*, 2006, *21*, 11–45.

Mazmanian, D. A., and Sabatier, P. A. "The Implementation of Public Policy: A Framework of Analysis." In D. A. Mazmanian and P. A. Sabatier (eds.), *Effective Policy Implementation*. Lanham, Md.: Lexington Books, 1981.

McLaughlin, J. A., and Jordan, G. B. "Using Logic Models." In J. S. Wholey, H. P. Hatry, and K. E. Newcomer (eds.), *Handbook of Practical Program Evaluation*. San Francisco: Jossey-Bass, 2004.

Melkers, J., and Willoughby, K. *Staying the Course: The Use of Performance Measurement in State Governments*. Washington, D.C.: IBM Center for the Business of Government, 2004.

Melkers, J., and Willoughby, K. "Models of Performance-Measurement Use in Local Governments: Understanding Budgeting, Communication, and Lasting Effects." *Public Administration Review*, 2005, *65*, 180–190.

Mohan, R. *Why Governments Need Performance Reporting*. Closing speech at the National Performance Management Conference of the Association of Government Accountants, Oct. 31, 2006, Schaumburg, Ill.

National Conference of State Legislatures. *Legislating for Results*. Denver: National Conference of State Legislatures, 2003.

Newcomer, K., Jennings, E. T., Jr., Broom, C., and Lomax, A. *Meeting the Challenges of Performance-Oriented Government*. Washington, D.C.: Center for Accountability and Performance, American Society for Public Administration, 2002.

Newcomer, K. E. "Using Performance Measurement to Improve Programs." In K. E. Newcomer (ed.), *Using Performance Measurement to Improve Public and Nonprofit Programs*. New Directions for Evaluation, no. 75. San Francisco: Jossey-Bass, 1997.

Perrin, B. "Effective Use and Misuse of Performance Measurement." *American Journal of Evaluation*, 1998, *19*, 367–379.

Perrin, B. "Performance Measurement: Does the Reality Match the Rhetoric? A Rejoinder to Bernstein and Winston." *American Journal of Evaluation*, 1999, *20*, 101–111.

Poister, T. H. "Performance Monitoring." In J. S. Wholey, H. P. Hatry, and K. E. Newcomer (eds.), *Handbook of Practical Program Evaluation*. San Francisco: Jossey-Bass, 2004.

Sanders, J. R. "Mainstreaming Evaluation." In J. J. Barnette and J. R. Sanders (eds.), *The Mainstreaming of Evaluation*. New Directions for Evaluation, no. 99. San Francisco: Jossey-Bass, 2003.

U.S. Government Accountability Office. *Performance Budgeting: Opportunities and Challenges*. Washington, D.C.: U.S. Government Printing Office, Sept. 19, 2002.

Washington Legislature. *Environmental Restoration Jobs Act*. Olympia, Wash.: Joint Legislative Audit and Review Committee, Nov. 1998.

Washington Legislature. *Linked Deposit Program Sunset Review*. Olympia, Wash.: Joint Legislative Audit and Review Committee, Sept. 1999.

Wholey, J. S. "Performance-Based Management: Responding to the Challenge." *Public Productivity and Management Review*, 1999, *22*, 288–307.

Wholey, J. S., and Newcomer, K. E. "Clarifying Goals, Reporting Results." In K. Newcomer (ed.), *Using Performance Measurement to Improve Public and Nonprofit Programs*. New Directions for Evaluation, no. 75. San Francisco: Jossey-Bass, 1997.

Winston, W. A. "Performance Indicators—Promises Unmet: A Response to Perrin." *American Journal of Evaluation*, 1999, *20*, 95–99.

RAKESH MOHAN is director of the Office of Performance Evaluations of the Idaho legislature.

MINAKSHI TIKOO is director of evaluation, quality management and improvement in the Connecticut Department of Mental Health and Addiction Services and assistant professor in the Department of Community Medicine and Health Care at the University of Connecticut Health Center.

STANLEY CAPELA is a senior director of quality improvement at HeartShare Human Services of New York.

DAVID J. BERNSTEIN is a senior study director at Westat in Rockville, Maryland.

8

This chapter provides reflection on and advice about the practice of evaluation in government policymaking settings, especially at the federal and state levels.

The Evaluator's Role in Policy Development

George F. Grob

Evaluators not only want to evaluate; they also want to be listened to. They hope that the data they relentlessly dig out of surveys, administrative files, and financial records; the insights they gain on exhausting trips to the field; and the creative solutions that miraculously descend on them in unstructured moments will inspire decision makers to adopt their recommendations and make the world better. This is especially true of those who evaluate government programs. What better way to make a difference than to enter the fray and work directly developing policy in federal, state, and local governments? The work is both rewarding and exhausting. But unless it is done effectively, it will mostly just be exhausting.

So what does it take to walk the halls of government agencies, legislative bodies, think tanks, stakeholder organizations, advocacy groups, and political parties with aplomb and success, and not lose one's soul in the process? It takes a professional command of the fields of evaluation and policy analysis, mastery of subject matter, character, and the ability to handle being simultaneously an advocate and an evaluator. These personal attributes are hard to come by, being built up slowly through learning and practice.

This may sound like cheap sermonizing, an easy stealing of the high ground, requiring no research, analysis, or insight, nothing more than the author appropriating to himself a comfortable moral perch high above his

---

The views in this chapter are solely those of the author and do not necessarily represent those of the U.S. Department of Health and Human Services or any component thereof.

WILEY InterScience® DISCOVER SOMETHING GREAT

colleagues. However, these insights were long in coming. It took thirty-seven years of government service, straddling policy and evaluation functions, for me to truly appreciate that who you are is just as important as what you do to be successful as an evaluator in the midst of policymakers. I wish I had appreciated this when I was just starting out.

Following are some reflections on these topics, from a career full of such work, including participation in over a thousand evaluations and numerous congressional hearings, budgets, policy papers, legislative proposals, draft regulations, press releases, and staff meetings. Fortunately, other evaluators more thoughtful than me have also applied themselves to understanding the connection between policymaking and evaluation and to the theoretical underpinnings of impact and persuasion. I will shamelessly draw on their published insights as well as my own experience.

Professional Practice

To be successful as an evaluator in the field of policy development, one must be eminently proficient in three fields: the subject matter of the policy under consideration (for example, health, education, transportation, housing, social security), evaluation, and the policymaking processes. Not much will be said here about the first two, since subject matter expertise is a lifelong pursuit, and the readers of this chapter are already steeped in evaluation. Instead, I will focus on the policymaking process and how evaluation relates to it. Nevertheless, it is worth dwelling briefly on the point about needing to be expert in all three.

Keeping Up with the Lobbyists. At the national and state levels, and probably also at the local level, the stakes in policymaking are high. Every word in every single line of a piece of national legislation or draft regulation is reviewed and ultimately painstakingly crafted with the full influence of representatives of industries that stand to gain or lose hundreds of millions of dollars, of workers whose jobs and family incomes are at stake, of activists whose causes are on the line. These representatives are often called "lobbyists" or "stakeholders," terms sometimes despised by government evaluators working in policymaking environments, who see themselves as the players with pure intentions and in possession of the truth. We will examine this premise more carefully in the next paragraph. For now, it is important to note that these representatives are very good at what they do. They have command of the three fields mentioned above, substituting only their personal profession (lawyer, economist, communicator, or something else) for evaluator. They know how laws are made; they know the ethical and professional guidelines of their profession; they too want to "make a difference"; and they work very hard at it.

The evaluator who wants to have impact in policy development must be as good at policy development as the paid lobbyists and advocates. The mere publication of "the truth" as the evaluator sees it is not enough.

The lobbyists are also in possession of the truth as they see it. It is a big mistake for the evaluator to dwell on his or her conviction that the truth gleaned from evaluation is pure, but the truth of others is tainted. First and foremost, this probably is not the case. The truth is hard to come by, and most participants in the policy process believe that they possess an important part of it, no matter how much they are paid or how they are motivated. Even more important, though, is the fact that they are competent, and the evaluators' truth will be of little value if they are outmaneuvered by the stakeholders.

Skills for Success in the Policy World. Mastery of the "how to do it" responsibility of an evaluator in a policymaking setting is fairly well established. I have written on this topic (Grob, 1992, 2003, 2004) based on my experience in the federal government. Jonas (1999) describes almost identical situations and methods faced by evaluators working on the legislative side of state governments, as do VanLandingham, Greer, and Bigos and coauthors in Chapters Two, Three, and Four, respectively, of this volume. All tell the same story. Successful evaluators work on topics of interest to lawmakers but bring new data and ideas in niche markets of policy development. They produce their reports when needed for hearings or markup sessions, usually under tight deadlines. As a result, their methods, since no perfect study can be produced under these conditions, must be buttressed by using several analytical approaches simultaneously, some involving hard data and others involving gathering viewpoints of affected beneficiaries, grantees, agencies, and the like. Such multifaceted approaches are persuasive to lawmakers.

Evaluators' reports are short, written in plain right-to-the-point language, with a few graphs or tables to emphasize important points. This makes them easy for lawmakers to absorb and draw on in their discussions with others.

Successful evaluators offer many recommendations or options to solve problems, not just one. They present practical solutions that can be implemented within current budget constraints. Nevertheless, their recommendations are often initially rejected by stakeholders, making legislators nervous about adopting them. But the evaluators make themselves available to answer questions, possibly doing additional work to fill in the blanks and respond to criticisms, plus listening to stakeholders' concerns and trying to respond to them. Eventually both legislators and stakeholders become more comfortable with the evaluators' ideas, and when the time is right, usually later in the legislative session, some of their recommendations, or similar ideas, may be picked up and included in bills to be passed by the legislature.

A fundamental tenet of all the successful practices of evaluators working in the policy field is that they look for ways to provide useful information to policymakers. What I have just described are practices commonly used by evaluators today. More innovative ways to connect evaluation practice with the needs of legislators are under development and hold promise for the future. These include use of an operational cost model, as described by Perry, Thomas, DuBois, and McGowan in Chapter Five of this volume, as well as forecasting methods described by Alter and Patterson in Chapter Six and performance measurement systems, as explained by Mohan, Tikoo, Capela, and Bernstein in Chapter Seven.

Personal Qualities. Engaged evaluators in fact know the legislative process as well as the stakeholders and legislators do. But in addition to knowing the ropes, they also have important personal qualities that facilitate their access to professional and political leaders of the legislature and key stakeholder representatives. First and foremost, they are knowledgeable and reasonable. They do not pander to others, saying what they believe others want to hear. Instead, they show through their conversation and written products that they understand the positions and concerns of lawmakers and stakeholders and that they have tried hard to answer their questions and find solutions that are acceptable.

They are also honest and straightforward in their speech and writing. Despite popular belief to the contrary, successful evaluators working in the policy arena achieve impact by convincing policymakers, not by deceiving them. They maintain important relationships by respecting others, not manipulating them. They do not hide things, as they have nothing to hide and because there really are no secrets in public policymaking. Sooner or later, every affected party gets a chance to weigh in and find out what all the other parties believe and have been up to. Evaluators do not work around the rules; they work them.

Evaluators working in these arenas also need a considerable amount of stamina. Policy changes, reflected in major legislation, budgets, regulations, and organizational alignments, occur only after many years of analytical explorations and consensus building. Yet the changes themselves may arise suddenly, in frenetic legislative sessions. As a result, evaluators wishing to have an impact on policy must have the stamina to work through both demanding aspects of the process: the long years of research, posturing, and compromising by policymakers, and then the chaotic, explosive conclusion, sometimes within the last days or hours of the legislative session. This requires a strategic outlook and the endurance to see the debate through to its conclusion.

Ethics

The minute one thinks of policy, the word *politics* comes to mind, and with it unsavory notions. Some evaluators wish to avoid policy development because they do not want to become involved in such tainted affairs. Perhaps, though, they should heed an evaluator's equivalent of the adage "Physician, heal thyself."

Standards of Practice. The successful evaluator in any subfield of evaluation practice must have a practical knowledge of and a habit of compliance with rules of ethical behavior. In recent years we have seen a maturing of *The Guiding Principles for Evaluators* issued by the American Evaluation Association (AEA) (2004) and guidelines published by other groups, including *The Program Evaluation Standards* (Joint Committee on Standards for Educational Evaluation, 1994); performance audit portions of the *Government Auditing Standards* of the General Accountability Office (U.S. Government Accountability Office, 2003); and the *Quality Standards for Inspections* (President's Council on Integrity and Efficiency, and Executive Council on Integrity and Efficiency [PCIE/ECIE], 2005). The *Quality Standards for Inspections* are used by evaluators in the various offices of inspector general within the federal government.

These guidelines combine rules of ethics with effective practice. That is, they show the evaluator not only how to behave properly but also how to get the job done right. This makes perfect sense, since it would be unethical to do a shoddy job. But the connection between "doing it right" and "doing what's right" also emerges because of the extremely nuanced situations in which evaluation is performed. For example, the fact that some evaluations need to be done fast gives rise to questions about the methods used. The fact that there may be no mandatory criteria by which a government program is to be evaluated gives rise to questions about how evaluators will choose the criteria they use.

The guidelines of the Government Accountability Office (GAO) and inspectors general go into considerable detail. These are particularly germane to the topic of this chapter because they are the guidelines that must be followed by government evaluators, many of whom practice evaluation in policy settings. For example, all of GAO's evaluation studies (which constitute the majority of what GAO does) are prepared at the request of and are reported to the Congress, which, by definition, make them highly relevant to legislators and therefore likely to be acted on by them. It would be well worth the time of evaluators with an interest in policy development, no matter where they work, to read these standards to learn what is expected in a policymaking environment.

It is not useful to discuss here all aspects of evaluators' ethical behavior. It is worth focusing, however, on three important facets that are particularly germane to the connection between evaluation and policymaking: independence, conflict of interest, and disclosure of evaluation information.

Dancing with Wolves? Some evaluators shy away from policymaking because they believe that too close an engagement with policymakers is inherently at odds with their independence. Some of the topics discussed earlier—doing studies at the request of policymakers or of known interest to them, attending to the concerns of stakeholders, using imperfect methodologies because of tight time constraints—send shudders up and down the spines of evaluators. Some of them believe that disengagement is the proper response; others believe it is irresponsible to avoid important evaluation work just because of the potential ethical traps.

There is no question that deciding how close to get to policymakers is a critical question for evaluators. Keeping one's distance may result in perfectly independent evaluations that are of little interest or relevance to policymakers. But getting too close raises the prospects of evaluators not wanting to hurt their "friends" by "telling it like it is," or, even worse, losing perspective or the ability to think clearly and independently. It is like walking a high wire: you can fall off to the left or you can fall off to the right; in either case, you are dead. But there is no shying away from this problem. To not walk that wire is to abandon all possibility of making an effective contribution to policymaking through evaluation.

The Jewel of Independence. What may come as a surprise is the fact that the evaluator's independence is of great value to the policymaker. It is true that some policymakers put pressure on evaluators, trying to divert them away from sensitive issues, asking that evaluation reports be released at times that are propitious for the policymakers, and depriving evaluators of data needed to complete studies. However, policymakers are far more likely to request an evaluator to do a study precisely because they want an independent view of things, because they really are interested in knowing how effective their program is, and because they would like to proclaim to the world that the results have been obtained by an independent source. An evaluator who has a reputation for selling out is not much use to a policymaker because the results are not believable. If a policymaker wants a slanted study, he or she can find someone to produce the study under contract.

So how does an evaluator maintain that independence while still consorting with policymakers? It is not that hard. The evaluator simply reinforces independence in dealing with sponsors. It goes like this. A policymaker requests that a study be performed by an evaluator. The evaluator agrees to consider the request. A meeting is held to discuss issues, methodology, and schedule. The evaluator begins by reminding the requester that the evaluator is independent and that the results will be what are found in the study. Still, the evaluator lets the policymaking sponsor know how useful it would be to understand the policymaker's concerns and interests. The conference ends with the evaluator promising to come back with a proposed evaluation plan, with a final reminder of evaluator independence.

The interaction between policymaker and evaluator can continue through the life of the project, especially at key points, such as the presentation of tentative conclusions or recommendations. An occasional polite reaffirmation of evaluator independence at these points seals the relationship with the policymaker in a way that makes collaboration productive.

Conflicts of Interest. The key to maintaining independence is for the evaluator to be independent. The evaluator must be constantly on guard against impediments to independence, such as conflicts of interest, biases, and family connections with stakeholders, etc. The impediments are spelled out clearly in the AEA, GAO, and PCIE/ECIE guidelines mentioned earlier. Evaluators should review these documents periodically to remind themselves of these provisions, and they must act on them. Evaluators make a big mistake in ignoring them. One may try to persuade oneself that one is not susceptible to influence from relatives, gift taking, or potential financial gain. But these and other impediments made their way into the guidelines because of the experience of lost independence of evaluators as a result of these factors in the past. In fact, the guidelines even emphasize the importance of avoiding the appearance of conflict of interest, even if no real conflict is present. The evaluator's reputation for independence, in addition to actual independence, is one of the personal qualities that makes him or her so valuable to policymakers.

Full Disclosure. This concern for the appearance, as well as the reality, of independence has a substantive side that goes deeper than the outward appearance. It has to do with the data and analytical underpinnings of the evaluation reports themselves. This involves the complete exposure to public scrutiny of the data and methods used in the study. A premise of work in the field of policymaking is that there are no secrets. Sooner or later every stakeholder will know what every other stakeholder is doing. If they do not know, they will demand to be told. It is commonplace for stakeholders to make requests for underlying study data under the Freedom of Information Act if the evaluator works for a federal agency. Except for personal information and other narrowly defined data protected by the Privacy Act, the requests will be honored. Furthermore, it is standard policy for many legislative evaluation offices to make their working papers public after the study is complete.

These are practical reasons for evaluators to be prepared to reveal the sources and details of their data and their methods. It would, however, be better to skip the consideration of what others might do or think and concentrate instead on what makes for effective evaluation. The principle is the same: there are, and should be, no secrets. Evaluators have no credibility if they make it difficult for stakeholders and policymakers to see what lies behind the evaluation results that could have a major impact on their interests. It makes sense to think of the product of an evaluation as a report and a box of evidence. From an even broader perspective, there is no better quality control system than the prospect that everything an evaluator does will be subject to public scrutiny, and such exposure should be welcomed for that reason.

The Evaluator as Advocate

Nothing strikes closer to the aorta of evaluator independence than an evaluator taking on the role of advocate. The dual role raises questions of how the evaluator will maintain independence. A nagging concern about this dual role may trouble even evaluators who are convinced that their role as advocate is legitimate. This concern about engaging in advocacy can be described intellectually, but its emotional content is also very high.

So sensitive is this question that it masks another, equally important one: how to do the job of evaluator and advocate effectively. It is easier to grasp the ethical issues by dealing with the latter question first.

In one sense, every evaluator who makes recommendations becomes an advocate, at least for that recommendation. However, this generally does not sound alarm bells. The issue arises when an evaluator takes a job with an organization with a mission and the evaluator's work is used to support the agenda of that organization. Let us use as an example the case of an evaluator signing on with an organization whose mission is to promote improvements in child welfare, and the evaluator studies various child welfare programs or proposed innovations. In this case, let us first ask how the evaluator can advocate effectively, and then consider whether that raises any issues about evaluator independence.

Influence by the Numbers. We are fortunate to have at our disposal several recent articles that systematically review evaluation and scientific literature on key aspects of this question and present conceptual frameworks to better understand the nature of influence and impact. Kirkhart (2000) provides a theory of influence involving immediate, end-of-cycle, and long-term influence, as well as influence stemming from both evaluation processes and evaluation results. Henry and Mark (2003) describe influence in terms of individual, interpersonal, and collective effects. Both articles are well worth reading, especially from the following perspective: the successful evaluator or advocate might well attempt to influence outcomes for social betterment using every path described in these two articles. In essence, Kirkhart, Henry, and Mark have provided handbooks on how to use evaluation to influence others and thereby achieve impact. Learning how to use all the approaches described in these and other similar articles will give evaluators far greater reach and success than even the passage of laws or the issuance of regulations. Of course, the evaluator must have rock-solid, worthwhile evaluations with findings and recommendations worthy of the effort to convince others to adopt them.

To add to this, I would also reemphasize some tactics mentioned previously: to offer many options for solving a problem, not just one; to limit the offerings to practical ideas that decision makers actually have the ability to carry out; to be persistent, offering not just one evaluation study but a body of work over an extended period of time in an area of interest to decision makers; to always be reasonable in dealing with others and to be open to their ideas.

Preserving One's Soul. With these ideas in mind, let us now turn to the issue of potential conflict between evaluator advocacy and independence. Obviously the evaluator-advocate should start by reexamining the AEA, GAO, and PCIE/ECIE guidelines. But we can go much further than that.

Henry (2000) introduces both ethical and practical considerations in warning evaluators against too much focus on the recommendations of a particular study and suggests instead that a substantial body of evaluations ought to address broader questions that help identify pressing social needs or the advantages, disadvantages, and ramifications of broad approaches to solving social problems. This more general approach puts the evaluator-advocate in a safer and perhaps more effective position. Few evaluators would deny the legitimacy of using evaluation to improve understanding of child welfare issues, and most would see the benefit of studies that address the broader issues. It would still be possible for evaluators to stray too far from independence in consistently advocating a certain general approach (for example, a liberal or conservative regimen), but if evaluators were to cross the line of independence, they would be far more likely to do so after becoming enamored with their own narrow solutions.

The excessive focus on a few narrow recommendations also interferes with effective evaluation and advocacy. It tends to lead to a closing of the mind that prevents the evaluator-advocate from listening to, understanding, and embracing solutions proposed by others.

A Healthy Distrust of One's Own Biases. In addition to focusing on big issues, it is important to adopt the practices and attitudes described in the previous section to preserve both the reality and appearance of independence. However, evaluator-advocates must also take the additional step of cultivating a certain wariness of their own biases and motives. This is not easy to do. For this reason, it is well worth the effort to go beyond the usual request for peer comments on draft evaluation products by seeking them from those with contrary points of view or political orientations. This will not only protect the evaluator from unconscious bias but will also facilitate the difficult exchange of ideas that is almost always necessary for warring parties to gain mutual understanding and eventual agreement on ways to bring about social betterment.

A Final Note

In preparing this retrospective on evaluators and policy development, I was struck by how many times I noticed that ethical behavior promotes effective performance. The preeminent example of this is the preservation of evaluator independence, which is a top ethical requirement and valued so highly by successful policymakers. The frequency with which "doing what's right" corresponds to "doing it right" was surprising. It is too late for me to benefit fully from this insight. I hope it will be useful to evaluators who are now fully engaged in or just entering the field and who hope to do good while they do well in their profession.

References

American Evaluation Association. *The Guiding Principles for Evaluators.* Fairhaven, Mass.: American Evaluation Association, 2004. Retrieved Dec. 31, 2006, from www.eval.org.

Grob, G. "How Policy Is Made and How Evaluators Can Affect It." *Evaluation Practice,* 1992, *13,* 175–183.

Grob, G. "A Truly Useful Bat Is One Found in the Hands of a Slugger." *American Journal of Evaluation,* 2003, *24,* 499–505.
Grob, G. "Writing for Impact." In J. Wholey, H. Hatry, and K. Newcomer (eds.), *Handbook of Practical Program Evaluation.* (2nd ed.) San Francisco: Jossey-Bass, 2004.
Henry, G. T. "Why Not Use?" In V. J. Caracelli and H. Preskill (eds.), *The Expanding Scope of Evaluation Use.* New Directions for Evaluation, no. 88. San Francisco: Jossey-Bass, 2000.
Henry, G. T., and Mark, M. M. "Beyond Use: Understanding Evaluation's Influence on Attitudes and Actions." *American Journal of Evaluation,* 2003, *24,* 293–314.
Joint Committee on Standards for Educational Evaluation. *The Program Evaluation Standards.* (2nd ed.) Thousand Oaks, Calif.: Sage, 1994.
Jonas, R. K. "Against the Whim: State Legislatures' Use of Program Evaluation." In R. K. Jonas (ed.), *Legislative Evaluation: Utilization-Driven Research for Decision Makers.* New Directions for Program Evaluation, no. 81. San Francisco: Jossey-Bass, 1999.
Kirkhart, K. E. "Reconceptualizing Evaluation Use: An Integrated Theory of Influence." In V. J. Caracelli and H. Preskill (eds.), *The Expanding Scope of Evaluation Use.* New Directions for Evaluation, no. 88. San Francisco: Jossey-Bass, 2000.
President's Council on Integrity and Efficiency, and Executive Council on Integrity and Efficiency. *Quality Standards for Inspections.* Washington, D.C.: President's Council on Integrity and Efficiency, and Executive Council on Integrity and Efficiency, Jan. 2005.
U.S. Government Accountability Office. *Government Auditing Standards, 2003 Revision.* Washington, D.C.: U.S. Government Accountability Office, 2003.

GEORGE F. GROB is an independent consultant. When he wrote this article, he was a senior executive in the U.S. Department of Health and Human Services.

INDEX

"A getting B to do H" proposition, 7, 9
Advocator role, 105–107
Alter, J., 4, 79, 88
American Evaluation Association (AEA), 12, 13, 31, 32, 103, 104, 106
American Heritage Dictionary of the English Language, 8
American Society for Public Administration, 73
Arinder, M., 28

Baumgartner, F., 29
Bernstein, D. J., 4, 10, 52, 89, 90, 97
Berry, F., 30, 31, 51, 54
Bezruki, D., 27, 51
Bias issue, 107
Bickel, W. E., 8
Bigos, Y., 2, 51, 66
Broom, C., 89

California Bureau of State Audits, 26
California Legislative Analyst, 26
Canadian Evaluation Society, 12
Capela, S., 4, 89, 97
Carter, R., 30
Chelimsky, E., 12, 21, 27, 29
Coffman, J., 2

Data collection, 90–92
Disclosure issue, 105
DuBois, E., 4, 67, 77, 102

Enlightenment evaluation use, 27
Epstein, D., 25, 26
Ethical issues: avoiding potential ethical traps, 103–104; conflicts of interest, 104–105; evaluator independence, 104; full disclosure as, 105; standards of practice, 102–103
Evaluation: four types of use, 27–28; of future impacts of legislation, 4, 79–88; impact on legislature actions by, 27–28, 41–49; legislative challenges addressed through, 26–27; reality check regarding politics and, 7–9; understanding the political environment of, 9–10*fig*. *See also* Evaluators
Evaluation independence/responsiveness: Idaho health and welfare management to maximizing, 18–19; Idaho public education studies on maximizing, 14–15; Idaho School for the Deaf and the Blind evaluation and, 15–18; ISIMS used to maximize, 19–20; value of maximizing, 11–13, 12*fig*
Evaluation influence: described, 2; four types of evaluation use contributing to, 27–28; on legislature actions, 27–28, 41–49; on state Medicaid policies, 51–65
Evaluation politics: "A getting B to do H" central to, 7, 9; maximizing independence from, 11–20; public policy evaluation environment and, 9–10*fig*; reality check on, 7–9
Evaluation Research Society Standards Committee, 80
Evaluation standards: Government Auditing Standards (Yellow Book), 13, 33, 35, 69, 76, 103; importance of using, 12–13; Program Evaluation Standards (Joint Committee), 13, 31–32
Evaluation utilization: barriers to, 31–32, 68–69; conditions and strategies affecting, 52–54; data creating indexes for, 32–33; overall use of, 33*t*–34*t*; overcoming barriers to, 69–70; performance measurement used to increase, 89–95. *See also* Legislatures; Public policy
Evaluators: advocate role of, 105–107; ethical issues for, 102–105; "how to do it" responsibility of, 101; independence of, 104; keeping up with the lobbyists, 100–101; personal qualities of, 102; professional objectives of, 99–100; skills for success in policy world, 101–102. *See also* Evaluation
Executive Council on Integrity and Efficiency (ECIE), 103, 104, 106

Fisk, D. M., 80
Florida Legislature's Office of Program Policy Analysis and Government Accountability (OPPAGA): background information on, 8, 51, 52–54; legislative Medicaid policies influenced by, 54, 55*t*–61*t*, 62–63
Frohock, F. M., 7, 9

Gilligan, T., 25
Government Accountability Office (GAO), 4, 13, 26, 31, 68, 69, 70, 80, 103, 104, 106
Government Accounting Standards Board, 89
Government Auditing Standards (Yellow Book): King County jail studies suing, 76; legislative evaluation offices' adoption of, 33, 35; overcoming barriers to utilization neglected by, 69; professional standards of, 13, 103
Government Performance and Results Act (1993), 90
Granovetter, M., 29
Grasso, P. G., 10
Greer, H., 3, 41, 49
Grob, G. F., 5, 52, 99, 101, 108
The Guiding Principles for Evaluators (AEA), 103
Guiding Principles for Evaluators (AVA), 13, 32

Harkreader, S., 2, 51, 66
Harvard's Kennedy School of Government, 95
Hatry, H. P., 80

Hendlin, R., 2, 51, 66
Hendricks, M., 30
Henry, G. T., 2, 5, 7, 106
Holt, R., 1
Horn, M., 26, 27
House, E. R., 21

Idaho Board of Education, 17
Idaho Educational Technology Initiative (1994), 91–92
Idaho Legislature, 15, 17, 19, 20, 92, 93–95
Idaho State Department of Education, 15
Idaho's Joint Legislative Oversight Committee, 14, 18, 19
Idaho's Office of Performance Evaluations: described, 14; health and welfare management evaluation by, 18–19; Idaho School for the Deaf and the Blind evaluation by, 15–18; Idaho Student Information Management System (ISIMS) evaluation by, 19–20; public education studies by, 14–15
Idaho's Technology Resource Management Council, 20
Ingraham, P., 26
Instrumental evaluation use, 27
Interpersonal influence, 2
Iriti, J. E., 8

Jail special studies. *See* King County jail special studies
Jennings, E. T., 89
JLARC (Joint Legislative Audit and Review Commission): background information on, 41; convergence of factors leading to legislative impact, 45–49; evaluation strategies used by, 41; Virginia Board of Medicine study by, 42–45
Johnson, J., 2, 5, 66
Johnson, R. B., 27
Joint Committee's *The Program Evaluation Standards*, 13, 32, 103
Jonas, R. K., 25, 27, 31, 101
Jones, B., 29
Jordan, G. B., 92
Julnes, G., 7

Key Evaluation Checklist (Scriven), 9
King County Auditor's Office: evaluation approach taken by, 67–68; evaluation independence and responsiveness of, 11; jail special studies series by, 70–76
King County corrections department, 67
King County Executive, 74
King County jail special studies: characteristics of, 70–71; phase I: cost study, 71–73, 72*fig*; phase II: jail costs follow-up study, 73–74; phase III: integrated security project and operational master plan development, 74–76; phase IV: monitoring implementation, 76
King, J., 5
King, L., 43
Kingdon, J. W., 29, 52
Kirkhart, K. E., 106
Klein, P., 31
Knight, J., 26
Krehbiel, K., 25

LAC (South Carolina): background information on, 51; legislative Medicaid policies influenced by, 54, 55*t*–61*t*, 63–65
Latham, S., 30, 31, 51, 54
Legislation impacts: benefits of assessing future, 79; lessons learned on evaluating, 86–88; limited past use of prospective evaluations of, 80–81; Minnesota's evaluation of NCLB, 4, 81–86
Legislature oversight offices: barriers to utilization strategies by, 31–32; challenges facing, 28–29; data creating utilization indexes for, 32–33; institutional design impact on utilization strategies by, 34*t*–35*t*; overall use of utilization strategies by, 33*t*–34*t*; strategies to promote evaluation use by, 29–30; survey studies (2004, 2006) on, 32; Yellow Book standards adopted by, 33, 35
Legislatures: actions on Virginia Board of Medicine by Virginia, 44–49; assessing future impacts of legislation by, 4, 79–88; using evaluation to address challenges facing, 26–27; examining impact of evaluation on, 27–28, 41–49; four vignettes on Idaho, 14–20; lobbyists working with, 100–101; public policy risks/challenges facing, 25–26; strategies to promote evaluation use by, 29–30. *See also* Evaluation utilization; Public policy
Linked Deposit program (Washington), 91
Lipton, D. S., 30
Lobbyists, 100–101
Lochetfeld, S., 28, 30
Lomax, A., 89

McCubbins, M., 26
McGowan, R., 4, 67, 77, 102
McKim, K., 27, 51
McLaughlin, J. A., 92
Mark, M. M., 2, 7, 106
Mayne, J., 89, 93
Mazmanian, D. A., 90
Medicaid policies: using evaluators' recommendations to improve, 8; Florida's OPPAGA influencing, 8, 51, 52–54, 55*t*–61*t*, 62–63; South Carolina's LAC influencing, 51, 54, 55*t*–61*t*, 63–65
Medicaid preferred drug list (PDL), 52
Medical Society of Virginia, 43–44, 48
Melkers, J., 89
Metropolitan King County Council, 71
Minnesota Office of the Legislative Auditor (OLA), 82, 83–86
Minnesota's NCLB evaluation (2002): background information on, 81; examining fiscal/programmatic impact, 4; findings of, 83–86; legislative request for, 81–82; lessons learned from, 86–88; methods used during, 82–83
Moe, T., 25
Mohan, R., 4, 5, 6, 7, 10, 11, 13, 14, 23, 52, 89, 93, 97
Mooney, C., 29
Mueller, J., 27, 51

National Center for Educational Statistics, 15
National Conference of State Legislatures, 13, 26, 28, 89, 323
National Legislative Program Evaluation Society, 32

Nelson, C. A., 8
Newcomer, K. E., 89, 90, 93
No Child Left Behind (NCLB): background information on, 81; examining fiscal/programmatic impact of, 4; Minnesota's evaluation study of, 81–88
Nobles, J., 87
Noll, R., 26
North, D., 31

O'Halloran, S., 25, 26
OPPAGA (Florida): background information on, 52–54; legislative Medicaid policies influenced by, 8, 51, 54, 55*t*–61*t*
Osborne, D., 26

Palumbo, D. J., 8, 9, 53
Patterson, J., 4, 79, 88
Patton, M. Q., 3, 8, 9, 11, 27, 29, 35, 52, 68
PDL (Medicaid preferred drug list), 52
Performance audits: data collection for, 90–92; Government Auditing Standards' definition of, 70; King County's jail special studies series on, 70–76
Performance measurement: to build evaluation foundation, 92; definition of, 89; increasing evaluation utilization through, 93–95; policymaker involvement in state-level, 93–94*fig*; understanding data collection for, 90–92
Perrin, B., 90
Perry, R., 4, 67, 77, 102
Poister, T. H., 92
Poland, O. F., 80
President's Council on Integrity and Efficiency (PCIE), 103, 104, 106
Privacy Act, 105
Process evaluation use, 28
Professional standards. *See* Evaluation standards
The Program Evaluation Standards (Joint Committee), 13, 32, 103
Prospective evaluation: lessons learned on, 86–88; limited past use of, 80–81; Minnesota's evaluation of NCLB, 4, 81–86; value of, 79
Public policy: evaluation environment of, 10*fig*; evaluator skills for working with, 101–102; four vignettes on Idaho legislature and, 14–20; influence of evaluators on state Medicaid, 51–65; legislative risks related to, 25–26; performance measurement for evaluation utilization for, 93–95. *See also* Evaluation utilization; Legislatures

Quality Standards for Inspections, 103
Quality Standards for Inspections (PCIE/ECIE), 103

Random House Unabridged Dictionary, 8
Rich, A., 26, 28

Sabatier, P. A., 90
Sanders, J. R., 93
Schneider, M., 29
Schwartz, T., 26
Scriven, M. S., 9
Scriven's Key Evaluation Checklist, 9
Shulock, N., 27
Sonnichsen, R., 29, 30
South Carolina Legislative Audit Council (LAC): background information on, 51; legislative Medicaid policies influenced by, 54, 55*t*–61*t*, 63–65
South Carolina's Medicaid, 8
Stakeholders: barriers to utilization by, 68–69; evaluators and lobbyists, 100–101; maximizing independence/responsiveness to, 11–13, 12*fig*; Program Evaluation Standards on meeting needs of, 31–32
Standards of practice, 102–103
Standards. *See* Evaluation standards
Sullivan, K., 5, 6, 7, 23, 93
Symbolic evaluation use, 28
Szabo, L., 44

Taylor, D., 9
Texas State Auditor, 26
Texas Sunset Commission, 26
Thomas, B., 4, 67, 77, 102
Tikoo, M., 4, 89, 97
Truitt, A., 2, 51, 66
Tubbesing, C., 26
Turcotte, J., 30, 31, 51, 54

University of Minnesota's Office of educational Accountability, 82
U.S. Government Accountability Office, 4, 13, 26, 31, 68, 69, 70, 80, 103, 104, 106
U.S. House of Representatives, 1
Utilization strategies. *See* Evaluation utilization

VanLandingham, G., 2, 13, 25, 26, 29, 69
Virginia Board of Medicine: background information on, 42; convergence of factors leading to legislative impact on, 45–49; JLARC study of, 41, 42–44, 45–49; legislative action regarding, 44–45; newspaper investigation of, 44; proposal for reform of, 44
Virginia Department of HealthProfessions, 44
Virginia General Assembly, 41, 42, 43, 45, 46
Virginia Hospital and Healthcare Association, 44
Virginia Medical Society, 43–44, 48

Wargo, M., 27
Washington's Linked Deposit program, 91
Web sites: Idaho's Joint Legislative Oversight Committee, 18; Idaho's Office of Performance Evaluation, 14
Weingast, B., 26
Weiss, C. H., 8, 10, 27, 28
Whiteman, D., 27, 28, 29
Whitsett, M. D., 10, 52
Wholey, J. S., 90, 92, 93
Wildavsky, A., 26
Willoughby, K., 89
Winnie, R. E., 80
Winston, W. A., 90
Wohlstetter, P., 26

Yecke, C. P., 87
Yellow Book. *See* Government Auditing Standards (Yellow Book)

Zajano, N., 5, 28, 30

Back Issue/Subscription Order Form

Copy or detach and send to:

Jossey-Bass, A Wiley Imprint, 989 Market Street, San Francisco CA 94103-1741
Call or fax toll-free: Phone 888-378-2537 6:30AM–3PM PST; Fax 888-481-2665

Back Issues: Please send me the following issues at $27 each
(Important: please include series initials and issue number, such as EV101.)

____

____

____

$ _______ Total for single issues

$ _______ Shipping charges:

Surface	Domestic	Canadian
First item	$5.00	$6.00
Each add'l item	$3.00	$1.50

For next-day and second-day delivery rates, call the number listed above.

Subscriptions: Please ___ start ___ renew my subscription to *New Directions for Evaluation* for the year 2_____ at the following rate:

U.S.	___ Individual $80	___ Institutional $199
Canada	___ Individual $80	___ Institutional $239
All others	___ Individual $104	___ Institutional $273

Online subscriptions are available via Wiley InterScience!

For more information about online subscriptions visit www.wileyinterscience.com

$________ Total single issues and subscriptions (Add appropriate sales tax for your state for single issue orders. No sales tax for U.S. subscriptions. Canadian residents, add GST for subscriptions and single issues.)

___ Payment enclosed (U.S. check or money order only)
___ VISA ___ MC ___ AmEx # _______________ Exp. date __________

Signature _________________________ Day Phone _______________
___ Bill me (U.S. institutional orders only. Purchase order required.)

Purchase order # ______________________________________

Federal Tax ID13559302 **GST 89102 8052**

Name ____

Address ____

____

Phone ____________________ E-mail ______________________

For more information about Jossey-Bass, visit our Web site at www.josseybass.com

Other Titles Available in the
New Directions for Evaluation Series
Jean A. King, Editor-in-Chief

EV111 Independent Evaluation Consulting, *Gail V. Barrington, Dawn Hanson Smart*
EV110 Pitfalls and Pratfalls: Null and Negative Findings in Evaluating Interventions, *Robert Nash Parker, Cynthia Hudley*
EV109 Critical Issues in STEM Evaluation, *Douglas Huffman, Frances Lawrenz*
EV108 Evaluating Nonformal Education Programs and Settings, *Emma Norland, Cindy Somers*
EV107 Social Network Analysis in Program Evaluation, *Maryann M. Durland, Kimberly A. Fredericks*
EV106 Theorists' Models in Action, *Marvin C. Alkin, Christina A. Christie*
EV105 Teaching Evaluation Using the Case Method, *Michael Quinn Patton, Patricia Patrizi*
EV104 International Perspectives on Evaluation Standards, *Craig Russon, Gabrielle Russon*
EV103 Global Advances in HIV/AIDS Monitoring and Evaluation, *Deborah Rugg, Greet Peersman, Michel Carael*
EV102 In Search of Cultural Competence in Evaluation: Toward Principles and Practices, *Melva Thompson-Robinson, Rodney Hopson, Saumitra SenGupta*
EV101 Co-Constructing a Contextually Responsive Evaluation Framework: The Talent Development Model of School Reform, *Veronica G. Thomas, Floraline I. Stevens*
EV100 Using Appreciative Inquiry in Evaluation, *Hallie Preskill, Anne T. Coghlan*
EV99 The Mainstreaming of Evaluation, *J. Jackson Barnette, James R. Sanders*
EV98 Youth Participatory Evaluation: A Field in the Making, *Kim Sabo*
EV97 The Practice-Theory Relationship in Evaluation, *Christina A. Christie*
EV96 Feminist Evaluation Explorations and Experiences, *Denise Seigart, Sharon Brisolara*
EV95 Responding to Sponsors and Stakeholders in Complex Evaluation Environments, *Rakesh Mohan, David J. Bernstein, Maria D. Whitsett*
EV94 Conducting Multiple Site Evaluations in Real-World Settings, *James M. Herrell, Roger B. Straw*
EV93 The Art, Craft, and Science of Evaluation Capacity Building, *Donald W. Compton, Michael Baizerman, Stacey Hueftle Stockdill*
EV92 Responsive Evaluation, *Jennifer C. Greene, Tineke A. Abma*
EV90 Evaluation Findings That Surprise, *Richard J. Light*
EV89 Evaluation Models, *Daniel L. Stufflebeam*
EV88 The Expanding Scope of Evaluation Use, *Valerie J. Caracelli, Hallie Preskill*
EV87 Program Theory in Evaluation: Challenges and Opportunities, *Patricia J. Rogers, Timothy A. Hacsi, Anthony Petrosino, Tracy A. Huebner*
EV86 How and Why Language Matters in Evaluation, *Rodney Hopson*
EV85 Evaluation as a Democratic Process: Promoting Inclusion, Dialogue, and Deliberation, *Katherine E. Ryan, Lizanne DeStefano*
EV84 Information Technologies in Evaluation: Social, Moral, Epistemological, and Practical Implications, *Geri Gay, Tammy L. Bennington*
EV83 Evaluating Health and Human Service Programs in Community Settings, *Joseph Telfair, Laura C. Leviton, Jeanne S. Merchant*
EV82 Current and Emerging Ethical Challenges in Evaluation, *Jody L. Fitzpatrick, Michael Morris*
EV81 Legislative Program Evaluation: Utilization-Driven Research for Decision Makers, *R. Kirk Jonas*
EV80 Understanding and Practicing Participatory Evaluation, *Elizabeth Whitmore*
EV79 Evaluating Tax Expenditures: Tools and Techniques for Assessing Outcomes, *Lois-ellin Datta, Patrick G. Grasso*
EV78 Realist Evaluation: An Emerging Theory in Support of Practice, *Gary T. Henry, George Julnes, Melvin M. Mark*